CALLED TO SHINE ACROSS AMERICA

RESTORING OUR ALLEGIANCE TO GOD!
A "PUT GOD BACK" MOVEMENT!

BY AUDREY MAULDIN

Called to Shine Across America

Trilogy Christian Publishers A Wholly Owned Subsidiary of Trinity Broadcasting Network

2442 Michelle Drive Tustin, CA 92780

Rights Department, 2442 Michelle Drive, Tustin, CA 92780.

Trilogy Christian Publishing/TBN and colophon are trademarks of Trinity Broadcasting Network.

For information about special discounts for bulk purchases, please contact Trilogy Christian Publishing.

Manufactured in the United States of America

10 9 8 7 6 5 4 3 2 1

Library of Congress Cataloging-in-Publication Data is available.

ISBN: 979-8-89041-055-9

E-ISBN: 979-8-89041-056-6

DEDICATION

First and foremost, I give God all thanks and glory for bringing me to write this book. He inspired dreams and visions, as well as the call to stand up in courage at a time and hour when things in this nation have appeared much darker. It's then that He has become a beacon of light in our journey, and as we adventure with His Holy Spirit, it's become an invitation into a divine relationship for us to share and extend to all who will listen. The Holy Spirit has been our mentor and greatest teacher, directing us on assignment to release His kingdom keys and revelation. He has done such a deep work in our hearts as a family that we feel released to help minister and write of His goodness. My whole life is devoted to expressing with every fiber of who we are, just how extraordinary our God is! The one who was, is, and always will be, forevermore…

I dedicate this book to my family, who have all been such a strength and support in my life. To my husband, Kendall, who is a great encourager and stands behind me or in front of me depending on the circumstance and is constantly by my side. I appreciate having a best friend, who is both an incredible listener and communicator. God matched our hearts and melted them together as I have received more of His amazing love through you! He knew that my visionary ideas would need an engineer to help design and set into motion every tool, structure, and idea to complete every blueprint He gave us. I'm so glad you're in my life. You make me want to be a better person.

To my children—Sophia, for having an eye to see the best in every circumstance and person. You have a way of loving so intentionally that it breaks off any lies that people believe when they think they are not loved. And my son, Enoch, for having enough passion to stand firmly for what he believes in, a seeker of great justice and fairness. I believe that by God's great grace, you will always find truth and follow Him with all your heart.

To my father and mother, Ernesto and Darlene, for their unlimited support and love. You two have always believed in all your children and have prayed powerful prayers to keep us on track and out of trouble. What amazing grace God had when He gifted us with such loving parents. You both live your lives so intentionally; I am inspired by how you reach out and become the love of God to everyone you know.

To my sister, Erica, who has been a rock that I could lean on through any trials I have had to endure. Praying for people and leading on the front lines requires great intercession coverage, and her prayers have always been timely and powerful. She is my leading best friend and has always been an amazing sister whom I've always looked up to. Her wisdom is beautiful, as she takes her time to listen clearly before she speaks, and she has been granted much authority for that. What a blessing to watch how God has preserved her and led her through so much in her own life. I look forward to continuing to see her step into everything that God has for her.

To my brother, Ernesto, and his beautiful wife, Jennifer—thanks for your hearts to pursue God as you serve others. Thanks for being such a protective brother. You always knew how to take me under your wing when I just needed reassurance. I'm excited to watch all that God continues to do in your lives.

To our loving apostles, David and Tracy Whittington, for standing strong as great leaders in our lives and shining in the radiant love of our Father. Our whole family gives thanks to God for bringing us to find you both and all our tribe at RHLC. You both are amazing examples of two people who live passionately and purposely for the presence of the Lord and connect so many others with His amazing love. He is your great reward. We hope we can be more like you two as we keep growing into all that God has for us.

Lastly, to Mama Darlene and Papa Roy, our beloved friends. We stepped together into a journey that would be a partnership of divine blessings. The Lord knew that we would journey together with His sweet Spirit into the heart of a nation that is crying out for His latter rain. You're both a gift from the Lord to our family. We continue to learn so much as we watch you both lead and grow leaders around you both. We love you.

ENDORSEMENTS

"Readers' hearts will be rekindled by Audrey Mauldin's encouraging, upbeat, and timely book *Called to Shine Across America*. Her stirring words will inspire readers to pray for a spiritual revival in the United States of America and the countries of the world. Audrey's passion and love for her country and her faith are evident, and they shine through in her writing. The need for a spiritual awakening in America and throughout the world is addressed in Audrey's writings, and her faith-filled prayers will inspire and equip readers to take part in a revival movement that will reverberate across our nation. Everyone who wants to comprehend the effectiveness of prayer and the effects of revival on the United States and other countries should read *Called to Shine Across America*."

—David Agyepong

Senior Pastor, International Life-Giving Church, Koforidua, Ghana, West Africa

"Audrey Mauldin is one of God's best-kept secrets, but not for long. Audrey is a gifted seer and prophetic teacher with revelation insight into the ways and purposes of God for our nation. There are many books written regarding our nation and the great revival harvest that is coming upon us, but none of them tops this one. Audrey and her family have traveled from state to state and have first-hand witnessed the move of God across America. You will be delighted and hopeful while reading the pages within. Your faith will be stirred and encouraged. I enthusiastically recommend this book, for its author is a firebrand with a pure heart and mind that points to our Lord and Savior."

—Tassi McGruder

TABLE OF CONTENTS

– CHAPTER 1 –

INTRODUCTION: AMERICA THE BEAUTIFUL

Inspired Letter to Our Nation

Oh, beautiful America, how precious you are in my sight! My land, which I formed from the beginning and made you a nation under my light.

A place where the union of hearts becomes one, forming an allegiance under my word. You loved me with an unmovable, unbridled spirit. Your founders sought ground and plotted out a place where freedom could ring so that all may come to know my radiant son, Jesus. They knew that freedom could not be bought but came at a price. One they were willing to pay with their lives, at times painting the flag crimson red and leaning on the atonement of the perfect Lamb who wiped away their sins so that they could build and start a nation under my righteousness. Leading into the blue stars, which held a promise given to Abraham long ago but is still being fulfilled as Jews and Gentiles become grafted into this story. So that today, you could hold a place as a nation known for its liberty. A land in deeper pursuit of a mighty God pouring out His glory upon all His sons and daughters. Knowing that the wonders released during Moses's age were only the beginning of greater things promised. All meant to be obtained by heirs of the promise, who hold in their hearts the memory of the Victor's crown gained at Calvary.

Your forefathers had come to know the cross and its purchased redemption. They longed to be witnesses of a generation that would come to the knowledge of my love. Evangelism became a tool as they sent many to other nations, sharing the gospel of my Father's remarkable love. In their hearts, His seed was sown and shared with many. These pilgrims had to leave all their belongings behind and journey to a place where they could lay out a new design. Leaving all fear of the unknown behind as they crossed aboard ships on voyages overseas that collided with uncharted paths. Their eyes pressed towards the mark of something greater, their hearts' determination holding on to the message of salvation leading into restoration.

And though I clothed you with fine linen and embraced you as my bride, your heart slowly faded and was gripped by the worldly seduction. Despite my blessings, you chose to look outward and become deceived by the promises of self-promotion. Not realizing that you lost your most precious prize when your eyes went from beholding your beloved, you then became disunified. As your desires now burn for more wealth, more individuality, and a new spirituality. I was left holding nothing more than just a memory of what you once looked like in your fading beauty.

Yet, I still have high regard as I am looking to reconcile you back into my arms. I want to hold you in my redeeming love, as I have already paid the bridal cost, and it was meant to be for a lifetime. I am not a generic God that you can throw me out when you think you have no need of me. I am, after all, the one who beheld you from the beginning as a creative thought and brought you from a molding slate, transforming you into something beautiful. So, until I am done, the story about you is still being written. There is still a remnant left among you with hearts as pure as virgins. Who long after me with all their hearts and will not let go until the great return takes place. Yes, the time of great humbling where every knee shall bow before my great splendor leading into an outpouring of my glory. Just as my prophet Hosea clanged to his bride despite her failure and shame, I, too, will write my name upon your hearts and bring healing to your brokenness. I am, after all, the one who called you first into forming, I have a plan, and it shall be fulfilled through you, *America the Beautiful,* as you return to me, your beloved first love! King Jesus!

God's Unrelenting Pursuit for His Nation: The Book of Hosea

Hosea 1:1–2 (NKJV):

When the Lord began to speak by Hosea, the Lord said to Hosea: Go, take yourself a wife of harlotry And children of harlotry, For the land has committed great harlotry By departing from the Lord.

He took Gomer as his wife, and she bore him a son, and they named that child Jezreel, which means I will avenge the bloodshed of the house of Jehu, and break the bow of Israel in the Valley of Jezreel, for all the horrible acts of murder committed on that land. Then she bore him a daughter, and they called her Lo-Ruhamah, which meant not pitied; this represented that Yahweh was no longer going to have mercy on Israel. A third child came, and they named him Lo-Ammi, which meant not my people; this indicated that God was no longer going to call them his own as he was fed up with their rebellion.

In Chapter 2 of Hosea, God describes the rebellion of His people as they went after their idols and sought after the Baals and the luxuries of the land and forgot about their God. The Lord, in His everlasting mercy, shows this undeserved favor as He calls them back into betrothal and into His righteousness and justice. He takes His people back into His faithfulness and reconciles them, and gives them new names, as in Hosea 2:21–23 (NKJV):

> "It shall come to pass in that day
> *That* I will answer," says the LORD;
> "I will answer the heavens,
> And they shall answer the earth.
> The earth shall answer
> With grain,
> With new wine,
> And with oil;
> They shall answer Jezreel.
> Then I will sow her for Myself in the earth,
> And I will have mercy on *her who had* not obtained mercy;
> Then I will say to *those who were* not My people,
> 'You *are* My people!'
> And they shall say, '*You are* my God!'"

In obedience, Hosea went to buy his bride back, though she had committed adultery, for fifteen shekels of silver. He took her and made atonement to redeem her and ordered her not to play the harlot any longer. There is no price we can place upon the ultimate sacrifice that Jesus made to purchase us from our rebellion and bring up back to His union. But in this same manner, He asks us to leave the past and the old man behind and allow ourselves to be unified with His love and His Spirit.

Hosea 3:4 (NKJV):

For the children of Israel shall abide many days without king or prince, without sacrifice or sacred pillar, without ephod or teraphim. Afterward the children of Israel shall return and seek the Lord their God and David their king. They shall fear the Lord and His goodness in the latter days.

He is calling us back to Himself.

I am reminded through the book of Hosea how God first loved us, to begin with. He has full plans for reconciliation to draw us away from our old mindsets and our old habits. He wants to renew the wineskin which we have so longed to prepare before Him. He made an example of Hosea by commanding him to marry the backslidden harlot, to display an example to His people Israel. I believe that imagery still holds true to today's age and is very applicable to our nation's disobedience as the Lord draws us back to His heart. In seeking the Lord and repenting from our old way, we are forgiven, and His love pours over us, so we will be praying His heart over our nation. I believe He still holds the door open for an opportune moment for our people and leaders to humble ourselves and pray so there is a true heart of reconciliation toward Jesus. We need to act quickly. While there is a season of grace, there shall be a time when He shall return to be united with His bride. When He returns, there shall be a time of great judgment. In John 16, verses 7–8 (NKJV), when the Lord Jesus was leaving His disciples, He reassured them:

> Nevertheless I tell you the truth. It is to your advantage that I go away; for if I do not go away, the Helper will not come to you; but if I depart, I will send Him to you. And when He has come, He will convict the world of sin, and of righteousness, and of judgment.

Are we willing to allow our hearts to be open to correction at a time when the Lord is cleansing and healing our land? I appeal to every heart as we keep on this journey together. Let's heed the words brought to us by the Holy Spirit. If there is time for preparations, let us not miss this mark. May we cry out, oh, Lord! Search us and shine your light over our hearts to restore us to a pure heart motive and allow your light to shine through us.

As we look at the beginning of this nation when it was first discovered, we find it already had natives living and caring for the land. Many had encountered the great spirit, who had been shown to many of the natives as the creator. Later as newcomers called pilgrims ventured across the oceans, they carried the message of Christ and ministered His salvation and grace. Their original intent came with pure heart motives. However, as many more traveled and viewed the land and opportunity to seize new territory, they became prideful and tainted by the desire to gain more possessions. First Timothy 6:9 (ESV): "But those who desire to be rich fall into temptation, into a snare, into many senseless and harmful desires that plunge people into ruin and destruction." So, the Lord sought to bring a redemptive plan before we even knew we needed a redeemer. The need for healing among the first nations people is an ongoing effort in order to have our nation cleansed and healed from the roots of wrongful entry. And as this nation became a place where many cultures would gather, it became formed on first the pursuit of godly principles and religious freedoms not offered in many other nations. It became a place where Jews and Gentiles could live as one under the Lord's principles and under religious freedoms to serve the Almighty.

May the heart of our nation become aligned with simple obedience to follow Christ and Him alone. That we will come into a knowing that it is through our time of difficulty and weakness that Jesus wants to be our greatest reward and strength. For such a long time, we have been boastful and trying to make a name for ourselves, calling ourselves the most powerful nation, yet our eyes reared off course, forgetting the prize and instead settling for unfulfilled promises. The ease of allowing a wave of pride to grow has now brought us into a slow fade and led to complacency. While the Father still holds His steady gaze upon the vision He had laid upon the lives that would spring forth faith like a seed that has been raised. All the passing winds, fires, storms, sands, and shifting tides keep rising higher to the surface with every generation passing. For what the heavenly witnesses peer out to see is found upon the rock. A seed that fell as it was trampled underfoot has now become the risen Son that lays His splendor on the nation that has lost its way and comes back to call on His name. It's His blood that spread out like a cover to adorn her out of shame and graced her with a white garment as He asked her to be His bride again.

And as she bends the knee before her beloved may she sing the song of Solomon 2:3 (KJV): "Like an apple tree among the trees of the woods, so is my beloved among the sons. I sat down in his shade with great delight, and his fruit was sweet to my taste." May she keep taking shelter and leaning into His protection. May she clothe herself with humility and find rest under His fair leaves, for as the times have gotten darker, she can still be led into His divine care. Where His loving mercy is unending, and His wisdom is given to help guide her. May peace be brought into her home and love be re-established as she finds her heart's true love, which has always been her true north. The one who leads her and guides her, the one who she first called her King. May she become a safe harbor, a place for both Jew and Gentile to become one new man in His sight and in His presence. Oh, what a delight and what a splendor that day shall be!

Our Pledge of Allegiance

On June 14th, 1954, our pledge of allegiance had a very important phrase added to it. This phrase is such an important image and echoes our stance as a nation: "Under God." The example of courage was demonstrated beautifully by Presbyterian reverend George Docherty, who seized a once-in-a-lifetime opportunity.

He was ministering at a Presbyterian Church in New York where President Dwight D. Eisenhower was in attendance. He had come from a Scottish background and was accustomed to hearing the allegiance of the phrases "God save the gracious Queen" and "God save the gracious King." This contributed to His awareness of the vacancy appearing over our national flag salute, as it had no mention of God at all. Though the Pledge of Allegiance had been written in the late 19th century by Francis Bellamy (the son of a Baptist minister), he had left out a very important aspect of the foundations which brought liberty into our founding Christian beliefs. As Reverend Docherty ministered a fiery message about the importance of having our nation be under God and adopting a pledge which states that, he convinced Eisenhower to add that address to the existing pledge of allegiance. Interestingly, though Docherty inspired the phrase, he was never invited to the actual ceremony dedication of the new pledge of allegiance to the flag.[1] This demonstrates that sometimes heroes can be unseen or unheard. In many instances, we are being called to be similar in areas where we may see that there is a vacancy that is allowing a huge void of God in places where we know that His name needs to be proclaimed. It's imperative that we begin to ask the question: Where can I help to advance and elevate the one name that is above every other name, Jesus? This is far more important than ever instead of trying to make a name for oneself. It's better to be a part of something greater, even when it requires our own dreams to be laid down to help build a kingdom-lasting structure.

A Nation Goes Off Course

Let's take it a step further. There are entire nations that have been formed with a God plan that have lost their way and taken the bait (desiring the appeals of the world) and are now in dire need of finding God again. Only He can help lead an entire nation into a place of humility and bring back its once-held pursuit of honoring and serving God. It begins with individuals finding their identity and sharing the Love of God in areas where they have taken victory over the enemy. When I speak of a put God back movement, I am talking about coming back to our first love and making God first in all that we do as an individual, family, and nation.

In this same manner, our nation, which once held such high standards of Christian and family values, has been undergoing its own identity battle and is in desperate need of a dramatic course correction. The foundational building bricks that once formed this nation have been shaken to the core and are in serious need of reformation. We must take our places and begin to enter intercession through the courts of heaven as we ask our Lord to release His grace over the seven mountains of influence, religion, entertainment, media, business, government, family, and education.[2] As we remain focused on Christ, the prize, the release of His wisdom, will set up a blueprint for restoration and rebuilding. Only He can bring healing to the level that our nation needs to be touched. It is time we move away from selfish ambition or world power; we must end the desire to choose temporal gain in wealth versus kingdom wisdom and advancement. Our nation will not build itself back up on its own strength. We need God. We can witness failures in various areas, such as the media giants and the social platforms that have chosen to feed the nation with a constant drip of fear, hoping that it will grip people into a passive state, especially the church at large when it should be speaking the loudest, in some cases it's been quiet and unseen. Perhaps, many are taking the non-conflict resolve, hoping that things will just keep getting better as they purely pray. At times they forget that prayer needs to be partnered with some obedience and on-time action. The most effective prayer is powerful when done from the right place of authority and asking God to help us partner our every action and step in obedience with His perfect movement to bring about the change He wants to release through us.

The enemy hungers after control of a society that is influenced by a slow fade of allowance, which has led to complacency or vacancy. Not all, but many have started to waiver. The fear of man has gripped them more heavily than the fear of God! We are seeing evangelists that are coming from different nations such as Africa, Europe, and Asia in order to help our nation come back to the truth and lead us out of selfishness and into reliance upon the one who formed us and knew us since the beginning of time.

Since he was thrown out of the heavenlies, the enemy has had a vengeance against the seed of God's created children, Adam and Eve, who fell into his illusion. Thus, his vendetta has long been expressed against the children of God. Today the battle continues for our children. It lies in the balance, beginning in the womb as worldly agendas infiltrate women's minds by giving the perspective that they have the right to choose when a life has already been conceived, and God gave that seed a right to life by His own breath. A child should be given the right to come forth into this nation and bring every purpose that has been written about him/her in the scrolls of heaven. This generation has been given a valuable assignment; therefore, it is being fought for before the children can come into agreement with God's plans. Those who are carriers of His glory are contending just for the opportunity to be born. What does this tell us? If Satan is after taking out an entire generation before their lives even begin, it's no wonder hell is shaking in their boots. They perceive that this generation is holding the key to something greater to come. An awakening is amid this remnant, one which will release a great resemblance to the kingdom sons manifesting Jesus because they take their rightful places in seated authority under God. Identity in Christ is the Key and unlocks the inheritance that will behold the greatest manifestations of the Son of God that this Earth has known.

The act of slavery, which has risen to an excruciating height where the young and weak have been exploited and forced into human trafficking. This is the work of demonic influences over laborers who bought into the darkest deception from the pits as they synchronized to hell's watch. In an attempt to play god over other lives, they have lost every empathetic emotion created to bring humanity into kindness and goodness. The mere image or thought of innocence being taken captive to be sold for financial gain is hard to comprehend. Perhaps it's because, as a mother of two, I could simply only choose the Lord's best for my own children. But I do know that in God's plan, He truly has a redemption plan. It is being woven into those who would listen to His Word. Yes, even those who have been found guilty of such a horrendous deed. It is never too late for as long as they stand breathing, we must reach out to those who would hear us bring even the worst offenses into His Son's radiant light, for only then can His grace and love peel back the hardening effects of hate. As a matter of fact, a repentant heart that truly surrenders can be rescued from the entrapment and enslavement of the evil one. Only Jesus can help a person who has been a victim of such a life. The prayers of our hearts must be with these that had no say but were wronged. Only the balm of Gilead can be placed over their minds, hearts, and bodies to bring a deep connection with heaven. Every day that passes us by, we need to fight for the release of these captives that are still chained and have no one who is looking for them because we are called to be that generation that will contend for the healing of those held captive.

As education of our young children stands at a balance, and indoctrinated theology is being served as a meal in order to bring a deterioration of their Christian beliefs, including acceptance of ideals that go against Christian values. Antichrist movements attempt to make Christ-centered faith seem old-fashioned and unaccepting of all people. We need to push back and raise children of light who hold all truth evident that Jesus is King, and His name is above everything created and yet to be created. They must know that there are truths established that are written and a compass that we must follow at all costs. We and our children must hold our ground and take our territory back. We must take our place at a time when the balances are set. We must stand and push back the deception and counterfeiting from our homes, schools, churches, and communities.

This is the hour we must stand up and speak loudly as we demand that God be put back into every place of authority and seat in our nation. We must take our places in the areas that God is calling us into. It's our only hope to gain back the fear and reverence of God's Word, which will lead us toward His truth and live under the right principles once again. We must let God live through us and become the change that we have been crying out for so long. His Word is the only one who can redeem our land. His name is Jesus! He desires to live in and through us to bring about the answers and the changes that are needed at this crucial hour.

Removing Principalities—Prayer for America

In recent visions, before embarking on our journey across the nation in intercession and proclaiming the kingdom's good news, I repeatedly saw that the Lord was taking principalities that had been rooted in position for many years as He was forcefully lifting them by the roots. They were little gods that had been allowed to take land not occupied by the children of God. The image of roots coming out of the ground that had been deeply rooted and hidden for so long, as they were covered in filth and were plucked out, a quick sense of reality came upon me. I knew that there had to be something replanted in their place. As the Lord has shaken everything that can be moved, He Himself, by the power of His right arm, is removing these strongholds.

He wants to set His order in place and release His anointing over His children, all who will come into His name. Kingdoms of this world shall be dismantled as God exposes lies and uncovers truths that shall change everything. He then spoke to my heart about the reality of needing to have sons come up into places of their rightful identity and take territories back for kingdom advancement. They can now take hold of these posts. Leaders are being called forward to arise. He is ready to equip and bless everything He has placed into their hands as they rise and says, "I am here, ready to stand, ready to move forward with heaven's perspective, as they carry the Lord's Dunamis Power and authority!" This will be a time when great deliverance ministries are coming to the forefront.

May our nation come into greater light as the truth about King Jesus is established to release His healing presence over all our land and people. A deeper heart pursuit begins in our own homes, with our families and children, and into our individual alter time with our King. It's imperative that we build him an altar and give Jesus the best part of our home, which includes the first fruits of our time, and worship Him at every available moment. We allow His light to come upon our hearts, minds, and souls and set us into a perfect rhythmic vibration so that everything in us is aligned with His perfect will and plans. The best part is knowing that as we humble ourselves and pray as well as turn from our wicked ways, as it is instructed of us in 2 Chronicles 7:14, we will begin to see a shift and turnaround as He releases a great measure of grace and forgives our transgressions and brings us into healing and restoration as a nation. Our hope is to be set upon the Mountain of the

Lord and always marvel at His gracious face and ways. He wants to bring us into His shelter and spread His blanket over our nakedness. That's what a true love does. It only wants the best and seeks out the best. It is patient and kind (1 Corinthians 14:4–8).

Prayer

Thank You, God, for aligning us all, as Your children, to have the right perspective of every situation and circumstance surrounding our lives. May we become engaged to let the light of Jesus realign everything in our lives, leading into every area of influence You have placed us into. Remove every stumbling block and expose the enemy. We repent of every sin we have stepped into, knowing or unknowing. We lay every burden at Your feet, Jesus. Forgive us for lukewarm living or passivity. Remove fear and reproach from our lives. We relinquish any covenants we've made with lies from the evil one. Lord, we stand under Your truth, and we received Your righteousness through Christ's finished work on the cross.

Open the dream realm so that all Your children can dream again, Lord. As the hidden things are revealed to Your people, limitations are broken off. May there be a renewing of the mind and a restoration of the soul in Your people.

As You release fresh fire baptisms, consecrate Your beloved bride, let identity be reshaped, and the image of Your Son Jesus be completely engraved upon our hearts and lives. May the value of life be seen as great and raise up defenders of the weak and of the innocent. Show us as a nation how to protect the unborn child and raise new standards within our legal constitutions. Show us how to love the orphans and bless those who need fathers and mothers. May we embrace single parents who just need a bit of help and support. Break the lies of false teachings and immorality that are driven by the antichrist spirit.

We ask You, Lord, to help bring back the heart of Your nation and its leaders and establish it right under God's shelter and abode. May it become a nation that runs back to the heart of the Father. Remind our nation of its first love, Jesus, as we humble ourselves before the mighty hand of our good Father. May Your name be proclaimed from city to city and from state to state unto the nations. We release this decree that Jesus is Lord over America! He is Lord over our lives and families. Amen!

- CHAPTER 2 -

A DREAM OF THE RAGING LIONS

Acts 2:17 (NASB, 1995):

"And it shall be in the last days," God says, "That I will pour forth of My Spirit on all mankind; And your sons and your daughters shall prophesy, And your young men shall see visions, And your old men shall dream dreams."

This was a scripture Paul referred to out of the book of Joel 2:28. After Pentecost, the Holy Spirit came over the men and women who were in the upper room awaiting the Lord's outpouring. They had been steady and tarrying together in prayer until the wind came forth, and the spirit blazed like fire upon their hearts. They were filled with such boldness and began to speak in other languages as the Lord released them into a higher calling. On that day, about three thousand were saved and added to the book of life as they came to know Jesus. Dreams and visions became a normal part of their life as they stepped into this place of relationship. Dreams reflect the significance of God's way of speaking to us from the beginning of Genesis to the end of revelations. There are many different reasons for dreams. We can obtain wisdom, purpose, warning, instruction/direction, understanding, and so much more.

October 5th, 2019

After a couple of days of fasting with an amazing partner this week, I dreamt on Monday the following dream. In my dream, there were lions all around us, all over the nation. They were hungry and ferocious! They were out prowling, seeking whom they could devour. Eating everyone and everything that came into their path. I went into a safe house or a hidden hut that appeared to be a warehouse. As I entered the house, there was a front room where a group of Christians were assembled to pray. They stood in a circle and held hands as they went into deep intercessions. I joined them, and we began to fervently pray in spirit. We were asking for mercy and protection during these attacks that were headed our way. We knew we needed help from the Lord. The nation was gripped with fear and needed to be rescued from the claws of the ferocious lions. We were praying without ceasing and trembling with reverence of God with all our hearts.

Then after praying for a while, they sounded the alarm and told us the lions were near, for us to assume our positions. We all ran inside the inner walls of the safe house and began to hide in the back rooms. We padded the doors and put things over the entryways for more weight. I had my husband cover windows and any areas that could be weaknesses. We noticed that as the lions got there, they began attacking. They used all their strength to attempt to enter and overcome us. These lions were ravaging everything in sight, leaving no one alive that they got. They were hungry. They had smelled blood and wanted more to devour.

I kept in sync with the voice of the Holy Spirit, who kept giving us our next way out. He showed me an attic door and said to go through there, so we moved quickly, and just when the lions were about to break in, we had already made our next escape. It continued in this similar way through a series of different doors and escape paths. However, he made way where there seemed to be none left.

The next room had a window that led out of the house and into an open field. I was prompted to move outside and go through the window, so I told my husband let's move out quickly. As we were climbing out the window, I looked outward, and about 200 feet or so were another two lions that were huge and saw us coming out. They were on my left side, and I looked over to the right side, and I saw a Rhinoceros right beneath a lower Valley. It was a field like one in Africa, but I knew we were in the US. I somehow knew that I needed to run towards the valley and into some brush that would hide me. I saw the lions prepare to launch towards us, and we began to run for our lives towards the lower valley leading up into another hill. They left the Rhinos alone and only ran after us, but we were given the strength to move faster.

A great wind came from behind us, and it accelerated our feet to run faster than ever before. It was supernatural. We were running so fast that we got to the clearing and came to the decision point of going up the hill. A few people met us there and gave us directions to another safe house up the small hill. So, I ran quickly inside and realized my husband was a bit behind. They held the door just long enough for us both to slide in, with only enough time to run inside before the lions got there. Quickly we resumed our next positions before we could pray as before. We ran inside as alarms sounded loud. The lions were there! Quickly I went straight into an open side corridor that had a ladder that had great openings from top to bottom. Somehow, despite feeling a bit exposed, I continued to crawl through the tight space.

I was climbing the ladder when I suddenly caught a scent of a wild animal. I looked up fearfully and saw the most majestic wild Lion with a mane that was so full and big. I knew that I could not escape this time. He was too close. As he looked down at me, his eyes were different. He had grace beyond my comprehension. He looked straight into my eyes as I shook in fear and spoke through his eyes as if into my thoughts directly. He said, "I have been with you all along, even when you didn't know I was there." I knew he was steadfast and loyal; this was my friend; he was protecting me and was not like any of the other little ravaging lions. I was completely overwhelmed by his love! I knew that my enemies had not been successful in getting to me because I had been safe under the roar of a much bigger Lion.

I somehow knew that this was the Lion of Judah! He was so mighty and majestic. His right leg alone held so much power and strength! I'm still seeing him in my visions! Just so overwhelmingly powerful! I just knew that He was loyal and saw me through every hard point I had gone through. He had never left my side.

I woke up and was in prayer about this dream and began asking the Holy Spirit for its meaning. I felt the Holy Spirit speaking in these areas.

I believe that the Lord is calling all intercessors into a much higher place in prayer for our nation. He said to assemble the prayer warriors and saints and begin to intercede for America. I felt the Lord saying this is a point of decision where my children must be praying all the time, the enemy has been raging and ravaging the land looking for openings so that he can destroy everything in his path, but God is saving those who will inquire of His plans to use them to change the outcome of this nation. He is calling us higher to stand in prayer to ask for advanced locations. To remain hidden in Christ as we intercede for our nation, its leaders, president, and security. God is going to give us a strategy against the plans of the enemy. He is going to keep us moving a step ahead. He is also going to release His power and presence over our lives to outrun the enemy as we stay in synchronization with the Lord!

We are going to come into face-to-face encounters with the radiant one, the most beautiful Lion of all. And as we do, He is going to reassure us that he is traveling alongside us through the journey and watching over us every step of the way! It is the roar of the mighty Lion of Judah that shall be heard and resound over our lives and over our nation. The established fear of God is going to bring a settling to the dispute of the little ravaging lions who seek to steal, kill, and destroy. As is written in John 10:10 (NKJV):

> The thief does not come except to steal, and to kill, and to destroy. I have come to believe that they may have life, and that they may have *it* more abundantly.

(A prayer 4:7–20)

Lord, break apart the little lions who are coming in the form of the Coronavirus and bring your children under your shelter as you fill them with the wisdom and presence of the Ruach of your breath. Help us to be used to extinguish the enemy's plans. I pray this in Jesus' mighty name, Amen!

(Updated Interpretation 3–5–22)

The original dream happened right in the precepts of our nation undergoing a dark pandemic that would stir the world into a place of fear and chaos. So many hidden agendas have come into play over the last few years, and our nation has been under serious demonic intrusion. In the last three years since this dream was written, our nation has undergone some major attacks which have impacted our society on so many levels. Through a widespread virus, the whole world had a huge setback in dealing with disease, which brought death and disunity to all the nations. These were the ravenous little lions that roared and were bloodthirsty in my dream. First Peter 5:8 (NIV), "Be alert and of sober mind. Your enemy the devil prowls around like a roaring lion looking for someone to devour."

In parallel to handling the virus, many disputes have entered our nation and our churches about how the virus situation was dealt with or not dealt with at all. Through this time, it has become apparent that the demonic kingdom has been creating prejudice and disunity among leaders on every level. Beginning at the heart of our nation and leading into even our familiar homes. Hence, I watched the intercessors gather at the points to pray because they needed to pray against the coming destruction from the lions. As they began, they prayed in the common place together, and as soon as the lions arrived, they went into the inner rooms to hide in desperation. I believe that the aftermath of the virus really brought many people to fear, making their homes become safe houses, but, at times, even their homes were not safe enough. It caused people on all levels to really have a look at what their inner hearts were carrying and allowed for deeper times of consecration to occur. Fear of the unknown and death gripped many people, so this drew them into their inner homes and into the closet of prayer and deep intercession.

As people humbled themselves to pray, there were distinct sharpening moments taking place for those who pioneered forward despite being threatened or harassed. Those who chose to press forward rose in light with creative ways to keep unity and stood in faith, believing God for a breakthrough that He would bring protection and pull them through the nightmare. Many lost loved ones to those lions, and some felt completely alone in the middle of the attack. It became a traumatic time of loneliness. As people kept to themselves and, at times, felt like the battle would never end.

The harassing roars of the lions in my dream were distinctively releasing great fear and trembling over the people. I believe that for those who pressed into the Father's heart by spending time at His altar, these are those who came into truly valuing His presence amid such chaos, they were able to live in peace and receive from His Word the comfort and healing that only comes from the Holy Spirit.

As I ran for a clearing through the valley, I saw rhinoceros, which could have had the following meanings; While some think and believe that in the Bible, a unicorn could refer to the rhino, perhaps it is because the word "rhinoceros" means "horned nose." All rhinos have horns—some have two, others have just one. *"Will the unicorn be willing to serve thee, or abide by thy crib [stable]?... Wilt thou trust him, because his strength is great? or wilt thou leave thy labour to him?"* (Job 39:9, 11, KJV)[3] In my heart, the Lord was saying I've got a unique opportunity that will be a time of strengthening for you, you will learn how to be strengthened in your walk with me, but I will lead you on a journey that is unique, and you must follow my lead as I bring You across the path.

As I saw what looked like a clearing and a valley in my dream that reminded me of Africa, it was a symbol that God would make a way to travel there during the pandemic. He sure made a way, and in the middle of the pandemic in early November 2020, he spoke to my heart and said, "plan your trip to Africa now." I immediately emailed my friend, who is a pastor of a beautiful church in Koforidua, Ghana, and promptly responded. Pastor David had just come back from the prayer mountain as they were earnestly seeking God. The Lord had spoken to them that they would be receiving visitors that were being sent from the Lord. I know that God held this window open as He had shown me in this dream the clearing which went right through Africa. God is using this nation to re-establish a reverence for God in our nation again. Interestingly, in earlier years, we sent great evangelists to bring Christ to the nations, and now these nations are standing in the gap through prayer and encouragement of the Saints. Leaders and pastors are pouring out all that God has shown them and investing in our people the gifts they have obtained while in relationship and communion with God. You will hear more about this faith journey as you read Chapter 5, the Mountains of Visitation, Atwea Mountain.

We went through a side entrance and found another place that was secured and protected. As we entered the next home, we pressed into prayer, but it was so sudden as the lions had begun advancement, showing us that the time had to be quick and we had to go straight in for protection. I believe that this is an interpretation of how quickly the assignment attacks are moving over the body. We have got to formulate and pray in every moment, not just in the times that we come together, but instead every moment, we must be praying in the spirit. In 1 Thessalonians 5:17–18 (MSG), pray all the time:

> Thank God no matter what happens. This is the way God wants you who belong to Christ Jesus to live. We must all pray without ceasing in the spirit.

Finally, as I came to encounter the Lion at the end of this dream, it was a holy fear that came over me. I knew with everything in me that this could be the end of my journey. However, he was not the enemy who had been encroaching. After getting past, staring at the majestic posture and beauty, I met a glance in his eyes. They were filled with all love. I knew this was the Lion spoken of in Isaiah 31:4 (ESV):

> For thus the Lord said to me, "As a lion or a young lion growls over his prey, and when a band of shepherds is called out against him he is not terrified by their shouting or daunted at their noise, so the Lord of hosts will come down to fight on Mount Zion and on its hill."

The interpretation received after prayer was that individuals across the nation would come into a face-to-face encounter with the great Lion of Judah, who would reveal himself to his children. The fear that once gripped them as they ran from the enemy's schemes will become a shifted encounter and instead will be lifted as they marvel at the mighty power that our God holds. He will put all our enemies under our feet and will conquer our fears as we give Him every area of our hearts. A deep consecration is coming over our nation, and the Lord has great plans to show up and rescue His Bride from the ravenous lions who have been hindering and scorching the land. It is not our Lord Jesus who came to steal, kill, and destroy—that is the enemy's doing. Satan is at fault for all the destruction and life stolen. Our King has come to bring life through Christ and to bring it in abundance. May we grab hold of the truth that is in His Word and be reminded daily of His goodness through grace and love. That is God's good nature.

Fear of the Lord

Over the last two years, God has been revealing His presence in a way that has been drawing me to an awareness of His all-encompassing holiness. As we have encountered Him at a place where the altar of God is inhabited by His holy angels and at times where I could do nothing else but allow His fire to burn over and through my soul in a way that levels out everything that doesn't, sound, look, smell, taste or resemble Him.

Proverbs 9:10 (NKJV):

The fear of the Lord is the beginning of wisdom, And the knowledge of the Holy One is understanding.

Webster's dictionary describes "fear" as "having a reverential awe of God." Often time, just thinking about everything He has created makes us stand at a place where we are able to marvel at His amazing goodness and see just how big our God is. He is the King and Creator of all things living and still being created. He is better than we think He is when it comes to love and gracious sacrifice. Everything about Him is holy, perfect, and pure. His light exposes idols that are hidden in our lands so that we can remove and break off idols in our hearts, homes, lives, and our nation.

In 1 Samuel, Chapter 5, the Philistines took the Ark of the Covenant captive and took it into their house of worship, where they gave offerings to their idol Dagon, meaning the crop fertility god. As the Philistines awakened the next morning, they went to their altar and witnessed that their idol god had fallen to the ground and lay face first beneath the Ark of the Covenant. They lifted their idol, and they placed it back up beside the ark of the covenant, and again, the idol of Dagon was found lying face down with its arms and head broken off with only its torso remaining. This time they were unable to just bring it back as fear overtook them. Severely the heavy hand of God came over the people of Ashdod, and they became afflicted with tumors. Fear spread, and they knew they couldn't keep the Ark of God in their city any longer. After confiding in their leaders, they decided to take the Ark of God to Gath, which also caused chaos within that city. After they arrived, great confusion came upon the people, and they, too, were afflicted with tumors.

The handling of the ark was shifted to Ekron, despite the uncertainty and confusion it brought with it. Rumors of the anger of God were falling upon anyone who was an enemy of Israel and chose to take in the ark. They assembled the Philistine leaders and demanded that the ark of God be sent back to its homeland with the Israelites. After all, it had been in the land of the Philistines for seven months and had killed and brought tumors upon the people, including five kings who ruled over the following five cities: Ashdod, Gaza, Ashkelon, Gath, and Ekron. According to the advice of their priests and sorcerers, these kings all made gold tumors and gold rats as an offering to God and sent them back upon the cart, which would be placed upon two milk cows, as the young calves were fenced back. These milk cows had never been yoked, as was prescribed by their priests. In a test, they would release the cows and see if they carried the cart towards Beth-Shemesh, which would prove that it was God who brought this heavy dealing with the people of the land. On the other side, if they traveled in the opposite direction, they would assume it was just back luck. The cattle did go the way of Beth-Shemesh and entered the land of the Levites. When the Israelites saw the Ark, they were able to offer a burnt sacrifice and rejoice together, for the Ark had returned.

God's wrath is nothing to be taken lightly. When His presence is involved, there must be a holiness that surrounds that move. Regrettably, many idols have been brought into our nation while many Christians have stood silent. The price for having these false idols enter cost our nation the innocent blood offered at the altar. It's not a coincidence that our nation has been plagued with new viruses that have been released into our land and have caused chaos and a scattering of people. Perhaps we can find wisdom in reading more of the scriptures and allowing our faith into new standards. The Lord's presence must become our resting place. We must become the present-day ark, carrying the Shekinah of the Lord's wonderful, exuberant, radiant glory. Then we can stand up against those false idols. They will have no power against the Blood of Christ. Just like Dagon, they, too, will find themselves on the floor with no hands (works) nor head (power/authority). They will be exposed and dismantled.

But are we willing to be offered up our lives for His, allowing Jesus to completely consecrate us into such a deep union. His sons/daughters of royalty, not of this kingdom or having no likeness of this world, but only of the heavenly dwelling. Even the Philistines understood the power of God's untamed love toward His people. Thus, His holiness became a stumbling block for those who had not yet understood who He was! They dared mishandle his presence and paid the price for that. His reverence precedes him everywhere he sends us.

We should be diligent in asking the Lord to seek our hearts regularly and have him expose if there are any idols in our hearts that would attempt to promote themselves ahead of His deity. If one is found, we should be quick to repent and turn away from our sins quickly so that His wrath will not be toward us or our homes or our nation. It begins in each of us, then moves outward into larger spheres where the Lord has given us the influence to impact and bring change in areas of the seven mountains.

In a later chapter of 1 Samuel 6:18, the people of Beth-Shemesh sacrificed the two cattle unto the Lord, but they made the mistake of looking into the Ark of God, which triggered seventy of their men to be struck down. (Some commentators believe that this number can represent fifty thousand.)[4] Instantly, they came to the awareness that they, too, were not qualified to be in possession of such a holy article. Chapter 20 (NLT):

> "Who is able to stand in the presence of the LORD, this
> holy God?" they cried out. "Where can we send the Ark
> from here?"

To whom should the ark go up from here?"[5] They eventually sent messengers to the people of Kiriath-Jearim, which was a city of forest given to Judah, and asked them to send someone to come and get the Ark and to move it out of their city. They sent someone from the house of Abinadab to take the ark into his home, and they consecrated his son Eleazer to guard the ark, and it stayed there for twenty years. Abinadab's name represents the father of nobleness[6], and Eleazer means my father has helped. As you can see, the house which was able to host the ark of the covenant had to be consecrated unto a deep cleansing. Abinadab knew the word. His reverence towards God came from knowing who the Father was as the Lord revealed knowledge of His intentions toward His people.

What would cause these Israelites to look upon the holiest chosen resting place, which had been covered by the angels built upon the mercy seat and had been sealed in the wilderness? Had they become curious about viewing the tablets that had once been touched by the finger of God, forgetting that holiness needs to be handled with great honor to guard the presence? After all, no priest, even after all his ritual cleansing, had ever gone to look inside the ark. They revered God's presence and knew that even Moses had to see God from behind so that he might not die. Or perhaps they had wanted to make sure that nothing had gone missing as it was taken captive by the Philistines. We may not fully know what prompted them to take such irrational steps, but it can be compared sometimes to how simple it is to grow complacent in how we honor and view the glory of the Lord in our churches and in our lives. Are we seeing our Father through the lens of Christ's love and sacrificial blood offering? As many of us seek to have face-to-face encounters, may we walk into His fire to allow our hearts to be purified and our hands to be made clean. Psalm 24:3–5 (NKJV):

> Who may ascend into the hill of the Lord? Or who may stand in His holy place? He who has clean hands and a pure heart, who has not lifted up his soul to an idol, Nor sworn deceitfully. He shall receive blessing from the Lord, And righteousness from the God of his salvation.

In some instances, the church has been praying and crying out for revival rivers to flow into their services. But the minute that the Holy Spirit starts moving upon the people, it's not always welcomed as a move that they expected because it is not viewed as ordinary. This has, unfortunately, led to many failed revivals. In a particular church we were visiting in Macon, Georgia, after worship and the word was shared, the presence was eager to move, but the spirit was being hindered. This brought such an imbalance, as there were fellow congregants that were eager and crying out for a greater move, and the minute that we prayed with an intercessor, we felt her joy overflowing and wanting to burst forth. She began to laugh out loud; the joy had been kept in for so long. I encouraged her in the Lord, we let joy come through us both, and at once the ongoing eyes that were on us were watching us with nodding displeasure. Laughter or joy offended some of the leaders. After we were done praying for the ones that were shown to us, the opportunity opened for us to pray with the pastor's wife. She seemed hungry for the spirit to move and kept saying that it was important to her. However, there was an environment being created by others that kept a close watch on any manifestation that they did not agree with. So, we were mindful and loving but really felt resistance in the realm of the spirit.

Later, we spoke to our friend who had sent us to this church, and her response surprised us when she said God has really been wanting to bring revival to that church, but they keep being visited and stopping the flow of the Holy Spirit and in separate occasions when God sent mighty rivers, they resisted the move and became dammed up. May we be more aware of how we are allowing the Lord to flow His rivers over our lives and how we let Him move through our church. We can cry out for revival with all our hearts and have pure intent motives, but if it is not being desired by the top of leadership, it will not be received when His outpouring is released.

The Bible is the most important thing to study, then partnering with Holy Spirit is imperative, as He is the one bringing us into the revelation and knowledge of everything we are reading. He wants to show that there can be manifestations of God's goodness moving into all our lives. That is also the way of gaining the true fear of God as He releases spiritual gifting that comes from the seven spirits of God. Isaiah 11:1–3 (NLT):

> Out of the stump of David's family will grow a shoot—
> yes, a new Branch bearing fruit from the old root.
> And the Spirit of the Lord will rest on him—
> the Spirit of wisdom and understanding,
> the Spirit of counsel and might,
> the Spirit of knowledge and the fear of the Lord.
> He will delight in obeying the LORD.
> He will not judge by appearance
> nor make a decision based on hearsay.

The fear of God is one of His spiritual gifts that comes over us as we receive the full baptism of the Lord. I love how King David could identify with the anointing in Saul's life, even though King Saul had been in pursuit after his life. When David and his men finally came to a cave, and his enemy was led right into his hands, he could have murdered Saul. Instead, he chose to only take a piece of his garment to show him how close he had gotten; however, a holy fear came over David. As King Saul was outside of the cave, David came out after him and before his men revealed to him that he could have snuffed out his light on that day if he had desired. David feared God's anointing and was not going to get between God's way or cease it from moving through anyone whom God had chosen. On that day, David showed his humility towards God's chosen vessel. He honored God so much that he refused to touch anyone that God had once chosen to lead into power. This was a beautiful honor that needs to be restored over our churches and nation.

Yes, God loves us with an unchangeable love. He called us first, and he wants us to be partakers of his beautiful presence. He is fearsome and lovely at the same time! We must yield every part of our members into this union with Him so that there is no opposition in us that would cause His presence to move away from us. We need to stay hungry and stay humble. As we draw near to Him, may we let Christ's love cover our sins, and may His holiness become our leading and our blessing. May we look upon Jesus as Holy Spirit opens our eyes to the revelation of God's Word and brings us into a greater and deeper understanding of His love. He has rescued us from a world of sin and brought us into a covenant that He made with His Son on account of us. All that is required is for us to say, "Yes, I choose you, Jesus," and believe in His finished work. We must depart from our lives of sin and step into His light so that we can walk in Christ daily. Freedom will come upon us as we let Him move concerning every part of our lives. We will then be granted access to receive our full inheritance found in God's Word, as we have faith to receive all of Him!

43

A Commissioning of the Lord - The Roar of the Lion of Judah

Tell them, tell them, tell them! These were the words that echoed into my heart and created an expanse beyond recognition in my soul. It became a commission ingrained into my spirit as the Ruach of the Lion was felt when his mouth opened, and he released a heated roar! I did not know that night in the fall of 2002 that as a young college student, I would encounter the King of the universe in such a way that he would leave me with an image that burned into my mind and heart, then cause me to turn away from the world of self-destruction into His presence and a place of healing and restoration. All because he showed up in a way that made every uncertainty, fear, and doubt become replaced by a reverence leading me into a perfect submission back to God.

It was my senior year in college, and I had just gone through some real struggles in finding my self-worth. It was chaotic trying to find my way in the middle of living in disunity, which I had created by taking all the wrong roads, each one pointing away from the Lord. I had mostly left God behind as a back-end thought and had embraced the momentum of party life, which brought with it instant friends and temporary vanity. An all too familiar void had been growing into a gaping hole in my soul. What began as a small vacancy had started to feel more like a black hole. Nothing seemed to bring me joy or gratification, especially relationships that all felt more and more dysfunctional. It was either someone I was chasing after that did not want to settle down or the opposite. I knew that my whole life was a measure of being off the tracks away from the truth, which God had intended in the first place. I was like a runaway train. Only this train had no rails or light to help me find my way back to its true intent.

On this night, I remember lifting a prayer of desperation and crying out to God. I had been dealing with deep depression and had been walking in an emotionless state for at least a few months. I remember saying to Him, "If you are the God of Abraham, Isaac, and Jacob, as well as Ernesto (my father), then you will show me you are real, show yourself!" I wept as I felt so alone and disconnected from reality. I had sunk into a deep depression and began to hate my life immensely. I knew that I needed to find help, a way out of this repetitive dark place. After weeping until my eyes were swollen, I began to lightly fall asleep. I could feel my spirit lifting from my body and instantly got taken up into a vision that resembled a feeling of moving outside of my body and turned into an out-of-body encounter. I entered a tunnel and was taken upwards; I felt my body being led by my hands first, and I could feel a physical wind going through my entire being. It began ascending, but I knew that I was being guided by something much bigger and stronger than I was. (Eventually, I came to find out this was Holy Spirit.)

I was moving very quickly and abruptly until I came to a stopping point, where I was allowed to move my head from side to side, and as I began to glance to the sides, I came to a stopping point near what appeared to be round windows on the side of the tunnel, each window had flashes of images. Each had graphic imagery of destruction being played out over the nation. I glanced to my left and saw homes being lifted by the wind, and tornadoes took up whole buildings and tore them apart. I saw grown trees being lifted by the root and broken in two.

45

Then I glanced to the right and saw forest fires consuming everything in their path, entering residential areas and burning homes down. I saw entire communities burning up by fire and people running for their lives in fear. Then I moved forward a bit and came to a window that brought much fear into my heart. It was a visual of people being tortured and beaten up to the point of seeing their teeth clench with pain. The hair on their heads was torn from their follicles, and the anguish that went through their facial expressions was horrific. I will never forget the smell of that corridor as their flesh burned and smelled like charcoal flesh, new since I had never smelled this before. Revelation 14:11 (NKJV):

> And the smoke of their torment ascends forever and ever;
> and they have no rest day or night, who worship the beast
> and his image, and whoever receives the mark of his name.

I felt the heat and fire as my eyes squinted, trying to shut down, but they were being held open. Every part of me wanted to turn away, but I was held in position staring at it, and despite trying, I couldn't look away. It was a glimpse into hell, and it was horrifying. I knew at that moment that I was being given a real look into what was to come, as well as a real place that lay in waiting if I did not change my ways. I began to say in my thoughts, *I want to get out of here. Please let me out. I don't want to see it anymore.*

At that moment, my feet were brought down under me, and I was allowed to stand upright. My whole attention was drawn towards a door across the path, which had a little peephole that allowed light to enter this dreary tunnel. I knew that I wanted to get closer to that light and see what was on the other side. I came close, and I leaned in to look inside the small triangular window. I immediately saw a beautiful park setting, with grass and flowers, as well as the sun shining brightly over the still photo. I wanted to get out and open the door that stood in the way between me and this image. My heart cried out loudly as I spoke, "I want to be there. I want to open this door and leave this place behind." But somehow, it dawned on me that this was an entryway that stood between two different times. I felt like the outside of that door held my freedom. It was life in the now, where things are still in peace while the Holy Spirit and grace are still upon the Earth. Allowing time for children to come to know Christ, I felt like the doorway was waiting for the Word of God that would release the seals to open the door. I shook as I knew what lay behind those doors was destruction in times of tribulation. Daniel 12:1 (ESV):

> At that time shall arise Michael, the great prince who has charge of your people. And there shall be a time of trouble, such as never has been since there was a nation till that time. But at that time your people shall be delivered, everyone whose name shall be found written in the book.

After this revelation came into my heart, I was immediately propelled backward through the same tunnel and went back in a similar position with my feet back and hands forward, and I was taken first through the tunnel by the wind, which positioned me back into my body, and I lay on my bed once again. A deep, heightened awareness came over me, but I still could not open my eyes. My body was lifted, and as my belly was lying facedown, my whole head came up, and my back arched upwards. Without opening my eyes, a full vision of Lion's head, which was only a couple of feet away from me, was revealed. It postured its body upwards. It was larger than any lion I had seen, perhaps because he was only about five feet away, and opened its jaws wide and let out a roar. The heat that came off Lion's roar went into my whole being, it was tremendous, and it brought everything inside me into a stance of awakening. A holy fear came over me as I felt my insides shaking. In that moment, I knew that I was beholding the Lion of Judah, and everything in me was in complete reverence of his mighty roar! I could only hear a resounding word come, which said, tell them, tell them, Tell them! Exodus 3:13–14 (NKJV):

> Then Moses said to God, "Indeed, when I come to the children of Israel and say to them, 'The God of your fathers has sent me to you,' and they say to me, 'What is His name? what shall I say to them?' And God said to Moses, 'I AM WHO I AM.' And He said, "Thus you shall say to the children of Israel, 'I AM has sent me to you.'"

Straight away, I was released, and I opened my eyes and directly jumped straight out of my bed. I knew that I had to call my parents and tell them what I had experienced. They both were joyful, as they had been praying that I would come back to the Lord. Together they prayed for me that night and reassured me that I was going to be alright. It was a new level of God that I had come into seeing and hearing. I knew that he wanted me to see that He was real and that His heart was calling me back to Himself. I knew that I had to turn things around in my life and begin to pursue Him, and that same night, I began to give Him every part of my broken mess so that He could begin the great work of redemption and restoration!

The most amazing thing about beholding the one that loves us, Jesus, is that it will leave an engraved image in our souls. He is so beautiful and wants us to encounter Him in His most wonderful ways. He is fearsome, and for those who find Him, He only wants us to seek out His enduring love and wisdom to bring a manifestation of His light into all this world so that it may expose and uproot all darkness. We hear of the Lion of Judah in Revelation 5:5 (ESV):

> And one of the elders said to me, "Weep no more; behold, the Lion of the tribe of Judah, the Root of David, has conquered, so that he can open the scroll and its seven seals."

We are told that the Lion was given the ability to open the scrolls, which will be done by His hand, as He can reveal to us those things which are coming in the days ahead. No one but the Father knows the day or time that Jesus will return. However, there are many signs that will happen before His return.

It's our desire to connect sons and daughters to their Father with His words, so we must keep speaking and teaching those things He has taught us through Christ. As we draw near to His Word, it will bring life and restoration, as well as release the captives from places of torment.

No person should be under bondage if such a high price was paid for every person to come away with Christ. The difference between them receiving their freedom can be found in the truth that they are set apart and already chosen. Have they received this invitation and responded?

I believe that this amazing encounter became the beginning of my true north calling, seeking all that had been lost. He was able to bring things back into order after I rededicated my life and began to pursue Him and all His ways. We were warned in Revelation 3:16 (NKJV), "So then, because you are lukewarm, and neither cold nor hot, I will vomit you out of My mouth. My reckless living was leading me into the very thing I did not want to become. And thus, the Lion's great roar brought me to my senses, trust me when His roar goes through you in such a manner it will shake everything out of you that shouldn't be there anyway."

Hell is a very real place, but it was not originally created for our purposes. It was intended as a place for the enemy. Matthew 25:46 (ESV): "And these will go away into eternal punishment, but the righteous into eternal life." We have the privilege through Christ to choose His righteousness if it is offered for our lives. When we believe in falsehoods, like preaching about hell not existing, we are not receiving the word in all its truth. I have seen measures or glimpses that I pray will never have to be shown to anyone. May we stay on the path that leads to our king's delight. May we be drawn into His purposes as we begin to see His kingdom's advance over our spheres and territories.

Let us pray:

A prayer for those searching and asking who they are in Christ: Father God, I lift the lives of those who are young and old, who would lift their voice to You in utterance today and say, "God, what is my purpose and who am I in You? What is my place, have I anything to offer that God can use?" May they find their lives as they reach up to You and give up everything that they held as their own truth. Align their gaze upon the one who is Truth. Amid giving you their heart and attention, may You recreate all that they have lost from the very beginning and fill them with hope, purpose, and vision. Let Your love pour over their hearts as they are drawn near to the Father.

Open the eyes of their heart so that they may call on You and allow You to be the center of all that matters. As they are searching to find who they are, may they find You, Jesus. May Your face shine over them and blessings come over them like a cloud by day and fire by night. Build a hedge over their relationships and have them be drawn towards those who fear You above anything else. If they are starting out in life as young adults, release Your wisdom to guide them as a friend and the Holy Spirit to guide their every step and decision. I lift those who are questioning if You are real up to You, Lord, and ask You to encounter them on your ground, shape their hearts and lives and move over them in new ways. Thank You, Poppa, for Your love.

CHAPTER 3

YOU ARE CALLED AND CHOSEN

God's Original Intentions (The Garden)

While you were still in your mother's womb, God knew you and already chose you.

He saw the frame of your body while it was still being formed, and by His Words, you were fastened together with every intricate fiber and knitted into a marvelous creation. As it was, He called bones to life, your vertebrae and bone structure became a temple woven together, and your organs were given water and blood to regenerate His divine order of life. He completed His work by wrapping you up with a cloth-like skin and breathing His breath into your lungs. He glanced over you with a warm Father's gaze and smiled as He breathed the breath that would catapult your spirit into its humble abode. Thus, you were brought into this world. Genesis 2:7 (NIV): "Then the Lord God formed man of dust from the ground and breathed into his nostrils the breath of life; and man became a living being."

Prior to bringing Adam into the world, God had taken a couple of days, six to be exact, to roll up His sleeves and work on separating light from darkness, sky and water, and land from seas. He set into their place (sun, moon, and stars) and created fish and birds, and land animals. His final plan was to place man in this spectacular garden to care for the Earth and animals and converse with God. What an amazing thought! Adam and Eve taking deep rest in His presence continuously and without hindrance walking in the cool of the day with God and sharing their hearts. Perhaps daily receiving God's wisdom about how to love and care for each other and the garden. And as they fellowship, they watched the green plants and animals be watered by the mist of heaven overlapping Earth. The unity of Earth and animals living in complete peace with man, what a beautiful place of rest that was, never worrying about what trap lay ahead. The word describes God walking with Adam in the cool of the day. What wonderful conversations must have taken place! The revelations of heaven released to this Earth must have been very rich and full, as peace remained over all that God had created. It was, after all, a place of friendship that He had designed where He could meet regularly with His children. It was a complete glory-filled realm where God took care of every need that man had or ever would have. It was a shelter where a man could behold God face to face regularly. Just as the land flourished with His glory, it was lush with every natural mineral and brought a bounty of food, water, shelter, and every good thing man could need. This image of the garden is such a brilliant reflection of the Lord's heart and intentions toward us all along. He wanted to be our protector and provider and journey with us to know us more and have us know Him. He wanted to shower us with His love and allow His radiance to become our everyday experience. His goodness was always a demonstration over our lives from the beginning and still flowing.

The Deception (A Lie That Came at a High Cost)

I could imagine after Adam and Eve were deceived by the serpent into an act of disobedience by taking the fruit that was forbidden, it caused a cataclysmic ripple into the once-perfect environment. Throwing things out of balance with the triune God, who wanted nothing more than to have complete transparency with His beloved children. The worst part of it all was that they already had everything they could have desired and needed, but with a seed of unbelief sown by the serpent, it landed on the unsettled ground. The test came down to whether they believed in God's goodness. Could God really be so good that He would hold nothing back from them? Unfortunately, they stooped into thinking that there was more available but not being offered to them. They already carried a full measure of the Father's love and blessings. Everything He had created belonged to them.

Instead, they chose to believe in the lie woven by the enemy, who had crafted a deceptive image, leading them to believe that God would withhold his goodness and not want them to have the ability to see as He sees. The deception grew into desire and then birthed forth action as they both disobeyed God's specific words. This disconnect and rebellion birthed the first sin, which closed a door and hung over their hearts a veil that kept them from the spiritual union. Unfortunately, even the gates of Eden became closed to them, guarded by an angel's flaming sword, for if they did not believe God, they might sin again and take from the Tree of Life, which he could not allow. However, even after Adam and Eve's failure, God still had a plan, for He knew in advance that He would pay for their sins and reconcile their hearts back through His son. After all, He is the one who sees in full and has already worked out the pathway to redemption through the coming of Christ, His only begotten son. Romans 5:18–19 (NIV):

> Consequently, just as one trespass resulted in condemnation for all people, so also one righteous act resulted in justification and life for all people. For just as through the disobedience of the one man the many were made sinners, so also through the obedience of the one man, the many will be made righteous.

In the same way that He promised redemption, He also called us first to Himself, away from our sin and unbelief. It's done both at the individual level and at the national level. In the Word, God spoke to Abram about making him a blessing and father to many. In Chapter 12 of Genesis, we read about the promise as he was told to leave his country and his family and go to a land that the Lord would show him. He was promised by God that he would be made into a great nation and become a great blessing. As well as through Him, all the families of all the Earth would be blessed. He also promised to protect him as if never allowing a curse against Abram. What an amazing friendship Abram had with the Lord! Of course, he still had to work out his faith through patience, endurance and keep the promises given to him by the Lord. This was evident when his wife was barren. Great challenges stood before him. His wife eventually attempted to help the fulfillment of the word by granting Abram her maidservant as a wife in hopes that the heir might be born through her servant. Unknowingly, that would bring much contention between Sarah and her maidservant when she bore a son named Ishmael. The doors of jealousy swung open. This also brought about a lineage that was not in the original plans. Thus, this opened a much bigger gate of disunity over generations of tribes who have been against the Israelites.

Again, this did not catch God off guard but instead demonstrated how perfect His redemption could still be, woven into the thread of missed human steps. Abraham sent Ishmael away; however, God was with the boy as he grew. Eventually, after trying to do it his way, he is called higher to wait upon the Lord's perfect timing, and thus, his son Isaac (son of promise) was born. Isaac would eventually have a son named Jacob, and this genealogy would branch into the lineage of Jesus the Messiah. God is so faithful to complete His Word and can do all things despite our shortcomings. Then, we see how He spoke to Israel at the national level in Exodus 19:5 (NKJV):

> Now therefore, if you will indeed obey My voice and keep My covenant, then you shall be a special treasure to Me above all people; for all the earth is Mine.

Deuteronomy 7:6 (NKJV):

> For you are a holy people to the LORD your God; the LORD your God has chosen you to be a people for Himself, a special treasure above all the peoples on the face of the earth.

God always wanted a relationship with us, and as we receive Christ, we can come back to that place of restoration and have those veils removed so that we can once again walk with Him in the cool of the day through the most beautiful garden found in our hearts.

An Ending Leading to a New Beginning

At the end of Dulcinea's life, the glory of God filled her little bedroom as she was ushered by the presence to be with the Lord. As her entire family witnessed her transition, it was both remarkable and miraculous. Death is not where I would personally choose to start but to truly give an account of a life well lived. One must look at the account of one from beginning to end, how the race begins, and most importantly, how it ends. Every individual on this Earth is on this journey from life to a greater life, one that requires guidance as we only have one opportunity to do it right. This is my interpretation of seeing my grandmother escorted out of this Earth and into her glorious heavenly body.

I've always been repelled away from death, especially funerals. I tend to find ways to steer away from anything that looks so much as even a memorial, however in this case, it was one event that I was not able to avoid, and I am glad I did not, or I would not have experienced the Lord in this great way. My grandmother visited us for Thanksgiving in 2005, and I remember fondly looking into her eyes and noticing that the white in her eye had begun to turn into a murky yellow. I asked my mother, is grandma alright, her eyes were glossy in warning, leading to a visit to the doctor's office that would not be favorable. She had a case of severely advanced pancreatic cancer with five months estimated to live. My grandma had gone from one day being healthy to lying on her deathbed by March 5, 2006, and her children/grandchildren were surrounding her as we read her favorite scriptures and did all we could to encourage each other in this mournful union. It felt like days, but it was only hours, she lay without speaking, and only a slight breath came from her weakening breaths as she inhaled, and her chest cavity was beginning to look frail. We were patiently praying and asking God to heal, as well as guide her home. Hospice had already sent us an in-home caretaker that could help explain the process involved in leaving our earthly shell. We consoled one another together as we told stories about Grandma and smiled. She had been a great example of a fiery intercessor who lived with great conviction and authority.

We reflected on the stories told of grandma walking into the hospital, into the bedroom where my dad, Ernesto, lay in a coma, as he had been in a car accident and was fighting for his life. She entered the environment with much authority, and as she spoke into the room, with one sentence, it shifted everything. She said, "Ernesto, get up now. Rise out of this bed in the name of Jesus!" Then, she simply walked away as if her part was complete. It was noted that my dad came up out of his coma within a few hours and eventually went on, a few years later, to marry her daughter, my mother, Darlene. After all, God knew that there were children waiting to be born out of their union. The books about their life together had not yet been completed, so God found Himself a vessel that would partner in faith with His purposes and release heavenly resolve into a decaying body. My grandma had enough faith to stir up the old dams of religious mindsets. She was used to God releasing waves of resurrection power, which laid the bridge to renewal and restoration for the next generation to come forth.

We reflected upon another occurrence earlier in her life, her daughter, my aunt Evelyn, had been injured in a head-on collision with a logging truck in her small vehicle. This near-tragic crash left her daughter with a broken right-side pelvis, and in order for it to heal, she was not allowed to walk on the right side at all. She was told by the doctors that she would be in a wheelchair for at least six months. She was in her recovery chair at home and getting accustomed to her new normal. Being wheeled in a chair seemed to be the only way to get anywhere at this time. My aunt speaks of a particular day when my grandmother was praying in the next room; she remembers listening to praise and worship music, and remarkably she saw the light in the room. Within the light, she could see the form of a person. Immediately, she jumped out of her wheelchair and ran into her mother's room. As she entered the room, she was overflowing with great joy and was shouting and dancing as she became filled with the Holy Spirit!" She told her mother, "Jesus healed me. I saw Him!" This was yet another wonderful time my grandma would witness the move of Jesus within her family. As Grandma partnered in prayer with all of heaven's authority and my aunt was restored instantly as she rose out of bed and began to dance around the room with Joy unstoppable because King Jesus had visited this house. She was restored completely and got her mobility back instantly. Praise God! I could imagine the host and myriads of angels singing that bright day as they watched a daughter arise into the light that she was called into by Christ our Lord.

The beloved disciple John understood how deep and wide the Father's heart was for His life. In Jesus's words, He records the following,

> You did not choose Me, but I chose you and appointed you that you should go and bear fruit, and *that* your fruit should remain, that whatever you ask the Father in My name He may give you.

John 15:16 (NKJV)

This was imparted over sons and daughters who knew who they were and who He is! I absolutely love John and how he focused on how much he was loved. He had a heart that beheld the one that was designed by his Creator and left a mark that set him apart. Many times, I have closely related to John's teachings because of the receptors that were rewired over my heart after being healed of a stoned and callus chamber. God, in His supernatural way, outstretched His hands and brought living waters. Behold! He gives us new hearts so that we can begin to receive all the Love that has always been flowing from above; just as a waterfall reaches everything downstream, so was my new outlook as I was awakening.

Grandma had been abandoned by the man she loved. He chose another family and began a new life while she was left to pick up the pieces and carry the load. And in carrying it, she did well. She became both mother and father to a strong son, David, and two sisters, Darlene (my mother) and her sister Evelyn, who would later become her helpmates. Dulcinea chose to make Jesus her best friend through and through, and I believe with every fiber of my heart that Grandma truly looked at God as her one and only King and Provider!

I would visit her time after time and have so many good memories of Bible books on her shelves, as well as sermons being played by evangelist Billy Graham and Jimmy Swaggart. Too many to keep naming, she kept up with those who loved the Lord. Having the right company meant learning from the wise who had gone ahead of her both in the Bible and in the mission field. She kept her Bible near her bed, and I still remember the frail pages as her fingers had swept through the thread of the fibers a thousand times. The Word had become her life, and His name was written upon her heart!

She loved to stock up her fridge room with so much food just in case the rapture came, and someone around her needed a helping hand. Perhaps it was a sign of enduring the great depression era, as piles of stored shoes and pajamas peered over a stack of never before worn piles of clothing neatly stocked in her extra bedroom. But she managed to always put away a few bucks under the mattress or in an old tin can. She was great at saving, a discipline that would leave a lasting great impression on her grandchildren when every need was met, even to the end of her life.

So, on that dreary day, I had just finished reading her favorite psalm. We kept alternating reading the scriptures to her as we listened to the rattling sounds coming from her lungs as she took weak breaths.

Then, loudly, we heard a knock on the front door. Who could be visiting at such a time? We were all silent, and as they opened the door, we saw my brother Ernesto enter and quickly go to her bedside to give Grandma one last hug. She had not woken up for hours and had been unresponsive until she heard His voice. He was the last grandchild there and the first grandbaby she had held. She was granted a last moment of strength and rose straight up and said, Ernesto, finally, you're here. Then she sighed with her last sigh, and she closed her eyes one last time. As we went back to praying and worshiping the Lord around her, it was a moment of awe. We couldn't believe that she had come back just to bid us all a final goodbye. Then within moments, the whole room shifted, and we could all smell a fragrant aroma entering the room. It smelled like the rose of Sharon, which was my grandma's favorite flower. It really felt like we had stepped into a garden that was filled with the aroma of roses, and a fresh wind blew this fragrance into her home. The confirmation was made by all of us present that it was the most amazing scent that came through her home, and it symbolized that her transition to heaven was taking place. We gathered in a circle and began to pray together.

To our amazement, three days earlier, before grandma had entered a coma, my mother, Darlene, and aunt, Evelyn, had been praying for her and tending to her needs, and as she was entering worship, she lifted her hands up and began waving them around in praise. Swiftly they saw a mist enter the room. It appeared like rolling smoke surrounding her bed coming up from the floor. That's when the most beautiful smell of the rose of Sharon came into the mist. The smell continued for a few days, even after she had passed on.

My aunt Evelyn, who is a spirit-filled believer, made mention to the rest of the family that the Lord had a message which was about to be released through His heavenly language, in tongues, and she said, "If anyone had an interpretation to please speak it out loud." Then she began to go into deep intercession and spoke in her heavenly language. Immediately as she was speaking, I felt a giant-sized hand come upon my chest and compress my heart between two hands. I heard a voice in my heart say speak, but I froze. All I could think of was, "Not I, Lord. I'm not sure what others will think. I'm the least qualified to speak for you!" I wasn't sure what to say as I hadn't heard the full interpretation yet. But again, the voice in my heart spoke louder and said, "Now, open your mouth!" My chest only grew heavier until I could barely breathe. I opened my mouth, and immediately, words started flowing, and I began to console the family through the word of scripture. I had never had such a thing happen before, and the very scripture the Lord gave me was from Psalm 139:12–13 (NIV):

> Even the darkness is not dark to You, the night will shine like the day, for darkness is as light to You. For you created my inmost being; You knit me together in my mother's womb. I praise you because I am fearfully and wonderfully made;

Isaiah 44:2 (BSB):

> Thus says the LORD who made you and formed you from the womb, *who* will help you: "Fear not, O Jacob My servant; And you, Jeshurun, whom I have chosen."

I also heard Jeremiah 1:5 (NIV):

> Before I formed you in the womb I knew you, before you were born, I set you apart; I appointed you as a prophet to the nations.

God reassured us through His message that our mother/grandmother was in His care, and she was free of all pain and suffering. She was in company and care of her beloved Jesus. She was now free and dancing in His splendor, doing things that she could only do in His garden, walking with Him as He shone His great light and brought her into a place where He could release her further into His delight. The Holy Spirit reassured us that Mom/Grandma was engraved into the palm of God's hand. The Lord did not take her away to hurt us, but her work here was complete. We were encouraged to continue with the work that she had been doing as it was now our time to complete the work left for us. After relaying the message, my whole body began to shiver with what felt like electrical flutters, but I was not cold at all. It was the opposite. I was completely excited and thrilled with the infusion of His Spirit and presence flowing through my whole body, beginning in my belly and flowing outward.

As a young adult, I was very grateful to have encountered God on such a level. I knew He was so much bigger, and there was more that He wanted to reveal as I kept growing with Him. I had gotten a taste of His overflowing, radiant presence, and it made me want to know Him more. In some ways, this experience catapulted me into a deeper pursuit of coming into knowing more about who I was in Christ. So, as a young adult, I gave God my heart and sought after Him diligently. I went to a youth group and spent time in prayer, long walks talking to God, and allowing Him to counsel me during some upcoming challenging years going into adolescence.

The Road Back: A Time of Healing

It did not come easy. Years after that, I would make many wrong decisions even after college, where I still had to learn by failure how it was more important to choose Jesus above this world and its vacant promises. It's amazing how the road that God had already made through Jesus would become an offered road back to reconcile my missed steps. In the beginning of these years, a rebellion had seemed so freeing from the legality of following the narrow path of religious legalism. It gave me a way out. Promised me a time of thrill and an abundance of friendships. However, left me weak, disunified, and unidentifiable. My character had become so shady, I could not look in the mirror and see the same person any longer that had once been used as an interpreter or mouthpiece for the Lord. I may have had many people who knew me, but none that truly cared about my well-being. I had become a shell of a person, and condemnation had really settled upon the borders and inner courts of my heart.

Jesus intervened and had to reinstate my old sunken heart and add to it new sails that would once again have the wind of the Holy Spirit direct me into the right course. This course correction was not a one-time happenstance. For me, it was a relearning of the bad habits that I had acquired and formulated, a laying down daily of my own will and desire that now needed restoration and healing work. Like taking a cog of a wheel and re-setting them into new grooves. God took me and began His great work. He continued His pursuit of my heart and continued to speak in all His love, despite all my failures. He reminded me of scriptures from Romans 8:28–30 (NIV):

> And we know that in all things God works for the good of those who love him, who have been called according to his purpose. For those God foreknew he also predestined to be conformed to the image of his Son, that he might be the firstborn among many brothers and sisters. And those he predestined, he also called; those he called, he also justified; those he justified, he also glorified. I am exhilarated that God answers our plea for help.

A Nation Step into Christ's Redemptive Love

Just as one life can be found and reconciled, how much more does He want to bring an entire nation back to Him! I am reminded of the request God placed on His servant Jonah, as he was commanded to go into Nineveh. At the time, it was one of the most wicked places. He was commissioned to preach the truth and release the words of life, which would lead them out of their darkness and destruction. Jonah did not want to go, as he knew that the Lord was merciful, and if they listened and turned in repentance, he knew that their city would be spared. He chose to run from his calling and the Lord. Instead, he headed on a boat to Tarshish. The Lord sent a great wind and storm amid his journey, and the seas grew tumultuous. Everything seemed to come against that ship, and Jonah knew it was his fault. That's the kind of wind the Lord will allow to come upon our lives. It could be tumultuous and even feel like chaos if we are not heading in the right direction leading us into our destiny. After lots were cast and results pointed to Jonah, he then revealed his disobedience before men and God. Immediately those sailing with him were instructed to throw him off the ship. Despite their uncertainty, the waves got severe and quickly beat down the sails. Thus, in great fear, they carried out the sentence and flung him overboard. Quickly the seas became calm in response to their sacrifice. Leaving no trace behind, only fleeting men sailing away from the darkest memory of raging disaster. In order to preserve his life, God sent a great fish to swallow up Jonah, and as he waited three days to be dissolved in its belly, in agony, he lamented in prayer. Could you imagine sitting at the bottom of a slimy fish, with your feet and hands stuck in fish goo? I'm sure that it was at that place that Jonah began to watch replays in his heart about his actual last commissioning by the Lord. His guilt and pain must have increased as he watched the end of his story be diluted into nothing more than a pile of rubble at the bottom of an ocean on a starry night.

The Lord gave Jonah a second chance and commanded the fish to spit him out unto dry ground. Then he called to him a second time and commanded him to go into Nineveh. This time, he did not hesitate. As soon as he arrived and began to minister in the city, all who heard the message in truth were convicted and began to repent. To think of the anointing that Johan carried that he did not even need to move with signs, wonders, and miracles, he only spoke the words of truth given by the Holy Spirit, and thus, the hearts of man became softened. He was able to release the Father's great salvation over an entire nation that chose to humble themselves instead of allowing their hearts to harden. I believe the Lord is giving our nation a chance to humble ourselves and listen to His prophets. They are being sent from the north, south, east, and west, all carrying a redemptive message leading our nation into deep repentance, and a turnaround is being released.

I pray that we become a nation that heeds the words of Jesus and does not keep asking for more signs after He has already given us everything. The sign that is raised is a merciful time of repentance, as His Spirit wants to have hearts restored and brought to His consuming love. We see what happens in Matthew 12:38 (NIV):

> Then some of the Pharisees and teachers of the law said to him, "Teacher, we want to see a sign from you." He answered, "A wicked and adulterous generation asks for a sign! But none will be given it except the sign of the prophet Jonah. For as Jonah was three days and three nights in the belly of a huge fish, so the Son of Man will be three days and three nights in the heart of the earth. The men of Nineveh will stand up at the judgment with this generation and condemn it; for they repented at the preaching of Jonah, and now something greater than Jonah is here.

Repentance begins at the heart of a nation.

My family was a witness, on the grounds of Washington, DC, on October 2017, when Awaken the Dawn had a national prayer day that lasted for four days. We walked around the nation's capital with our two children in a stroller and watched as tents representing every state were propped up and manned for worship 24/7 for a whole week leading up to this event. We witnessed an old and young generation merging as they manned posts held for specific states, worshipped in their style, joined hands, and began prophesying over those passing by. Oh, what fire we gazed upon that night! As we saw that there remains a remnant more alive than ever before, hungrier to see the Lord rise over our nation as the first sunrise. Their hearts' pursuit was pure as they sought after God, crying after the Father's will and peace.

Then, on September 26th, 2020, through prayer, fasting, and repentance, our nation sought the Lord for a great return. We stood on the grounds in Washington, DC, when millions took part in this significant day and night movement, which is now opening the doors for the third great awakening to spring forth. There was so much oil in the presence of God for a nation that yields in repentance for all our national sins, both hidden and exposed corruption. There were seven trumpets blown over the nation of America by a Jewish Rabbi, and with it came great anointing and breakthrough. To this moment, as I think about what took place on this holy ground in our nation's capital, I still get the chills thinking of how perfectly the Lord moved through the ministers who poured out the Word and decrees in mighty power. The first trumpet was for the unleashing of the purposes of God through His power. The second trumpet was for the power of Jericho, breaking down walls of idols and strongholds. The third trumpet was for the power to return and repent, a turning back to the Father. The fourth trumpet was for the power of redemption and salvation over the nation and the Earth. The fifth trumpet was for the power of anointing, the power of victory, and the book of Acts. The sixth trumpet was for the power of revival and the outpouring of the Holy Spirit, for showers of the Holy Spirit. Finally, the seventh trumpet was for the will of God to be released on Earth. A final trumpet was sounded by every leader that was given a horn to blow, symbolizing a sealing of the return. The rolling waves of the Lord's glory kept resounding outward by these prophetic actions, and the blessing of God from the house of the Levites was graciously spoken over our nation. Oh, what a marvelous day to have been a witness!

It has been about three years since the great return, and the Father has been faithful in that in just the last year, 2023, there has been a momentum in the highest courts towards overturning Roe Vs. Wade. Life is being fought for in the womb. Thus, changes are being made despite the movement of dark agendas that still exist. Our Father is raising a higher standard as His children take up posts in lands that are filled with trenches. He hands them shovels and rods of authority to build back and put God back into every area that still echoes His name. All creation shall bend its knee to the Father who lifts a city from the ashes and into His beauty.

In May of 2022, we also had the opportunity to attend The Send at Arrowhead Stadium in Kansas City, MO. This was a powerful move of intercession, and a call to action, calling the Body of Christ into interceding for the nation and carrying the love of God into the world. It was evident how God had connected the dots with the events leading up to this point in time, drawing so many closer to Him and His purpose for this land and hour. We were stirred in our faith, ready to go anywhere He sent us as a family, along with the thousands that were there receiving the same encouragement.

What will we do with these messages that lie before us, as prophets are being attacked at a time that we need the word in all its truth? And because so many have been falsely speaking with no fear or reverence of the truth, it's led all to be viewed as one voice, failing to have risen discernment for those who are, in fact carrying the message leading to life. This is the hour we must arise to know our Father's voice. We cannot miss it. It's the difference between life and death. As we look to Christ's redemptive offering, may we join the ones that are now being sent. Yes, a new era has arisen, one of a likeness of His rising sons. We must take our places and run with the wind and fire of the Lord. No fear gripping us or holding us back, only a reverence leading us to stand for His justice and His purity as His Spirit baptizes all hearers into His Word.

His Words are being made known to us through divine impartation and revelation. We can have the heart of our eyes open to His light by the Holy Spirit. In dropping our agendas and being willing to take His message to every dark corner of our nation, we begin to see power manifest. A land that once sent out its light barriers to all the nations is a land that is now more in need of the Father's holy consecration. It begins with us accepting all of Him and leading others to hear His truths. May we come back to Him, may our knees grow weak before Him, and may the great return produce a great turning back to the

71

Father. Leading us into an effective time of sending sons and daughters into the fields which are ripening into the whitest maturing. This is a time for a grand harvest. Can you see it?

– CHAPTER 4 –

BREAKING OFF FEAR

The Environment Created Through Fear

Fear can create environments all around us; however, we can choose how we will react to the circumstances that cause fears to spring up in times of uncertainty. Animals are sensitive to fear that is projected through prey or hosted by their environment. Just riding a horse for a couple of hours has opened my eyes to how connected an animal can be to its environment. If I flinched and held his reins too hard or felt uncertain of his masculine posture, it then caused that animal to stir around me and attempt to take the lead, as he sensed any weakness in me. One bumpy trail in Florida led me into a tug-of-war with a horse that had quite a personality. He wanted me to know that he was in charge, and I was not quite aware of how to put him in his proper place. I allowed fear to enter and thus allowed the intimidation of the animal the right to bring fear. Ultimately, we had a great guide who was able to help rein in the horse until we were able to get back to the stalls. Any wild animal, after all, is a creature of the wild, but in the same manner, the dominion that Adam once lost in that sacred garden has been restored by the price Jesus paid.

I've often wondered about how Daniel managed to overcome the lions in the dark dungeon. In Chapter Six of Daniel, we hear about a trap that the governors and satraps lay before King Darius. They had conspired a rule that there could be no worship or prayer to any other god outside of the king. Otherwise, if found guilty, they would be thrown into the lion's den. After hearing this, Daniel heads home and opens up his window in the direction of Jerusalem, and begins to give thanks to his God, just as he had done since earlier times. These men assembled around his home and found him praying, and thus, they turned him over to the king and forced the rule to be applied as the law could not be reversed.

Daniel was a man of great honor as he walked in a way that pleased the Lord. Thus he had found favor with God and the king. Ultimately, he still had to pay the price for breaking the law, and so it came to pass that he was thrown into the lion's den. The king's final words over Daniel before he sealed the den with a purposed stone was, "Your God, whom you serve continually, He will deliver you" (Daniel 6:6, NKJV). Perhaps even King Darius had seen a faith that was unmovable in Daniel as he watched him live a life that was completely consecrated. It's awesome how even an unbeliever could imply trust in God of another by watching the dedication of his unhindered heart. And as that stone was rolled over the opening and the light became dim, moving into obsolete, complete darkness, he was left facing his greatest fear! Or not? Perhaps, it could be that Daniel had been healed of all his fears prior to being sent into the pit. Could he have been blanketed by an immovable God that held him up by His banner of love surrounding him with an image of what heaven would look like in complete peace? A place that is void of fear and of pain or suffering. If so, the wild lions would have had no ability to sense any environment around him, but instead, His peace could have very well become their open ground for deep rest.

Or could it even be that he had already died with Christ as he entered that den, so he was granted access to overcome the harassment of death that the enemy had intended for his life? Could it be that God had given Daniel an early glimpse into knowing that there was a destined Messiah who would be able to conquer death after three days of being in a tomb? After all, Daniel had studied the word and knew the prophecies and knew that in God, there were no limitations. See, the enemy seeks to devour each one of God's called vessels. Stay alert! First Peter 5:8 (NLT):

> Stay alert! Watch out for your great enemy, the devil. He prowls around like a roaring lion, looking for someone to devour.

I could only imagine what occurred inside that den on that night. Could it be that as angels surrounded Daniel that they kept him encircled with a sphere of peace, or could they have lifted him up and translated him from that place into an encounter with heaven? I imagine that whatever did happen, it was incredible. Daniel had found his peace with God, man, and creation, and just like Adam in the garden, he was stepping into a deeper union with all of God's intentions and promises. Early in the morning, the king went in haste to open the den and lamented, hoping to see his friend still alive. As he called out eagerly to his friend, he heard Daniel speak, saying,

My God sent his angels and shut the lion's mouths, so that they have not hurt me, because I was found innocent before Him; and also, O king, I have done no wrong before you.

Daniel 6:22 (NKJV)

Oh, what release and joy must have washed over King Darius. Not forgetting he himself had prophesied that Daniel's God would be able to save him. This must have been a time of great celebration for the king and for Daniel. He came out of that lion's den and walked right into a promotion. God wants us to relinquish all our fears. Then we become free of all things leading to death, and we can truly take our seats as God's sons. His inheritance is already awaiting the heirs to rise in a time of adversity and trust that He will deliver us out of the lion's den.

Regaining Our Voice (Pushing Off the Bushels)

Are you fearful of speaking about your faith and love of Jesus? Sweat and tears ran down my face as I stood in a quiet downtown office suite, with countless listening ears pressed toward us, like radar receptors zoning into our rather awkward conversation. Panic struck me when my co-worker David looked at me after he had opened a lengthy prayer of introduction to the Lord's holy presence and led me before the great altar, then introduced me to Jesus and said here she is to make her request before you. Then silence fell over the whole room. I could see little eyes peering above the small cubicles as fellow co-workers were being entertained by my cowardly stance as I stood there petrified, shaking. I wanted to say so much to God, but I could only let out very few quiet words, which to my pardon, were still received. I squeakily spoke out before the Lord, "God, I really want to have the courage to speak about you to others and have my faith be on the outside, not just the inside. I want to be free of this fear that grips me and does not allow me to speak about who you are." Then, I paused, and my friend David ended the prayer with a bold stance and closed us out as if we were in an auditorium in the middle of a stadium of revivalists. I was somewhat relieved that the prayer was over, but at the same time really saddened, as I could barely muster up the courage to pray in such a meek manner. Thank goodness that Jesus was alright with my shy request. My prayer had indeed touched His ears.

A few weeks later, it would become a huge turning point as I would lay my fear down on an anointed altar in Ohio. My co-worker, Cheri, had countless times mentioned to me the many intriguing truths about the revival that was spreading throughout the nation. I listened minutely but tried my best not to get involved in loud conversations around our highly political and official work environment. Red flags were sprouting up like alarms all around Cheri and all her radical Christian friends. I knew that even if my heart enjoyed spending time listening to her theories, I wasn't making any friends in the sphere of leadership that peered into hearing some of the conversations. One day she went as far as inviting me to one of their revivals in a nearby state. Something about this invitation made me uneasy. A huge part of me wanted to come, but a part of me was fearful. As I fought with the decision, I knew that I truly needed to become alert and awake.

Too much fear had crept into my heart, and I was slowly becoming an inward Christian soldier, unable to move with the rhythm and sound of my Father's drum beat. Desiring and longing to have the freedom to share what I felt on the inside, especially about my love for Jesus. So, I convinced my husband, Kendall, to join us, and we both found ourselves inside our friend's van headed for Ohio.

I should have known that it wasn't going to be an easy seven hours. Every part of the journey became an excruciatingly painful experience. I started having a headache on my way there, and it only got worse. Cheri prayed in intercession as she drove. She knew that I was going to reach higher freedom. We finally got there, and to my surprise, the line awaiting entrance was quite long. It was a whole new world of excitement as I waited to get into the church auditorium. Not too often had I seen this many people filled with an electrical charge, desiring to be in God's presence. It was somewhat contagious and made me feel like I was getting ready for something amazing. It was a couple of pastors coming to visit, and they were part of the Bay of the Holy Spirit revival in Mobile, Alabama. The young pastor was surely carrying a fresh fire for our nation.

On the first day of the gathering, I really enjoyed the worship, and it was my first time witnessing worship under such total freedom. I really wanted to be as free as a bird to make my own song before my father, but instead, I felt hindered. After the word was released, I looked around and saw many people being touched by the presence. It was going out in waves, and one of those who got touched by the Lord was my husband. He received electrical currents running through his whole body, and he violently started to shake. It was amazing watching all of heaven stamp him with a signature of authentic love. I stood behind him and pleaded with God to touch me as well. I did not want to leave that place the same as I had come. So, after the service ended that night, I went to my hotel room and was upset. I conversed with God and said, "Why would you only choose my husband and not bless me as well?"

I remember receiving back a very loud message in my heart, and I knew it was from God. I heard, "Wife, you might not even get a touch! You asked me to fill your husband, and so I did. Now you are angry and upset." It immediately dawned on me that I was wrestling with words from my creator, who is not capable of lying, and I could not fathom trying to win this debate, so I quickly submitted myself and asked for forgiveness. I remember weeping and saying, "Father, I'm sorry, I do not need a touch. I love you just because you are good! I will go tomorrow and just worship you, even if I don't feel a thing. You are so worthy of my praise." That night, I submitted my heart before a mighty God. I also realized that I needed God to help me in my submission. I had found a blessing in my husband already, and just as he received the blessing over his head, it would pour down onto his whole body and cover me as well, for we are one body. I, too, received that oil of gladness.

I awakened with a new heart and prepared myself to be a worshipper the next day. The expectation was different. My hopes were already in Him, all clinging to the finished work of the cross. Whether I got to encounter a touch or not, I was so grateful for just being found in Him. I could truly just worship Him with all that was within me. There was freedom in just being under such a sweet banner that morning. After the fiery evangelist ministered, the Lord released a revelation fire of His presence over the entire auditorium. Immediately, my heart began to pound and ache, it was as if the chambers of my heart were opened to deeper truths, and my soul was being called into a new depth of freedom.

An invitation went out for us to have our eyes placed upon our king, Jesus, the one who was standing there with Him. Immediately, my eyes were opened, and I could see Jesus through the veil of tears that were pouring out of my eyes. Oh, what a glorious sight! I watched as He walked over the stage and came down the stairs where I was standing. As He came close to me, my whole body shook, and I hit the ground. I let out a sharp squeal, and I felt a deep sweep as though the Holy Spirit had just swept everything out of me that was not ever meant to have any grip or hold on my heart. All I could do was kneel and cry in the posture of kissing the feet of Jesus. I was so grateful for the extreme exchange that was taking place. I felt like the load of heaviness was just removed from my shoulders, and I just wanted to weep in deep joy. I knew that all religious mindsets and setbacks, as well as lies, had been dismantled. I was solely in a relationship and a union with Christ.

The next thing I knew, I was rising from the floor, and it truly felt like the old heart had been turned to ash and rubble and was left lying on the altar. I was now standing as a new creation. I could hear the following scripture in my heart, Then He who sat on the throne said, "Behold, I make all things new." And He said to me, "Write, for these words are true and faithful." I was then filled with the spirit of joy, and great laughter came over me. It eventually turned into a mighty wind of dance. I began to dance in a way that made the scriptures about King David come to life. It is described that he danced so intensely that he lost his clothing as he was completely in freedom before the Lord. I did, however, manage to keep all my clothing intact. But spiritually, every stench of grave clothing came off. The invigoration of coming into that level of freedom was captivating. There was nothing I could want more than to just surrender my whole body and heart to the Lord. This was all just the beginning of what would become the best freedom that I could have stepped into by God's grace.

On my return trip back, it became very evident to our family and friends that something new had taken place. The moment I stepped into our apartment home, I recall looking across the room and catching a glimpse of my husband, Kendall, but he looked completely different. There was a light that surrounded him, and it beautifully wrapped around his body as a warm blanket. Immediately I knew that my eyes had been changed, I could see him in a fragrant color, and it exuberated the feeling of love. We began to take our regular walks around our community parks and trails. Along the way, we stopped with many people and shared the beauty and love of our good father with them. There were no walls to hinder the love that was being poured through us, and we saw hearts melt into God's hands as we came into hearing and ministered regularly.

As I returned to my office, it was not immediately easy, and there was no reception awaiting us. Instead, my supervisor was not expecting what would happen next. After sharing with her the beautiful encounter with Jesus, as well as my new heart for His awakening and, of course, an invitation for her to receive Him also. It became a point of contention as I was warned regularly not to share my faith in boldness across the open areas of the office. This, however, did not stop or damper the new fire God had kindled in me from being shared on the streets of Baltimore, Maryland. A group of us would take our lunch hour and walk the streets and lead as many as were sent to us to the Lord. What a time of growth, restoration, and healing this became. A time I came to feel like nothing was impossible with Christ.

This setup became an open-door invitation to understand more about the kingdom realm. His Holy Spirit drew me into a new desire and regular entrance, and connecting to His presence became a destiny roadmap. I wanted nothing more than to know Him and have Him become made known to everyone around me. My prayer began to be fervent in asking God to wake me up and shake me up. Jesus was so present in me that I began to surrender every aspect of my life to Him. He began to quickly shift things into the right place and order.

Receiving a Prophet's Reward

A train that has been traveling off-track eventually gets to a point where its wheels will no longer carry the load. The off-road eventually leads to bumps and rocks that have not before been familiar to its design, and those small wheels that were intended and created for the purpose of a track will be off balance and kilter. At times all that is needed is an active word that is sharper than anything else to flip your train back unto the right rivets and create an acceleration into the realm of His kingdom that can only be imparted through His divine Word by the Holy Spirit's breath.

On August 30, 2018, a prophetic message awaited me one morning as I opened my social media and began to read. It was interesting and inviting, as this person apparently had insight from God and knew more about me than I knew about her. It was, in some way, drawing me towards wanting to find out more about how could her connection with God have given her this knowledge. But instead of giving it any attention, my first instinct was to close the inbox, moving on to other areas that felt a bit more familiar. Until, over the next couple of weeks, I gently forgot and kept moving forward with other tasks. A gentle leading came over me as the Lord interjected and began to speak over my heart, "Why won't you give this woman a chance if I'm the one who sent her into your life?" So, in following the Lord, I messaged her back in the next week, and she invited me to her women's meeting in a small ecclesia (home church) in Gaithersburg, Maryland. The arrival came one fine Saturday. I drove up to this house not knowing a soul, and having my husband on speed-dial, letting him know my whereabouts, just in case I went missing, he would know where I last checked in. I had butterflies in my stomach, and at this point, I really wished that I had invited someone to come with me. Perhaps I should have put aside the feelings of foolishness as if I was believing or being hopeful that this was really God making His move, and underneath it all, it could be a bad setup.

To my surprise, as I stepped into the house, I was warmly greeted by a couple of women that were in deep preparation, as I had arrived early. They were putting out snacks and preparing the small speakers for the worship that they were going to have. It was surprisingly inviting as the women introduced themselves, and as I met the prophetess of the house, I felt completely at peace as I met her and felt the Lord's cloth of humility and love wrap around her. How she spoke and interacted with the ladies in the house was beautiful, she approached each person with such deep concern and respect. Her house consisted of a few strong backgrounds of denominations, some Catholic, some Pentecostal, and some Baptist. It was a precious union, but they all shared the same heart of the father and the same Spirit.

Tremendous impartation was received from this gathering, and I began to see an image of something that I felt that God wanted me to see. There was much intimacy and a stronger relationship with this small group of women meeting in a home that they kept calling their ecclesia. This was a similar blueprint to the way the church originally began, as disciples were positioned by the Lord. They visited homes and grew believers until they outgrew their meeting places and kept expanding. The word went out from region and spread to nations as everyone took personal responsibility to share their testimonies of the blessing of Christ coming into their hearts. The Greek term for "church" is *ecclesia*. The word can be separated into a compound of two segments: *ek*, a preposition meaning "out of," and a verb, *kaleo*, signifying "to call"—hence, "to call out."[7] I really felt that God wanted to show me a blueprint of a new model of church in a new era, one

BREAKING OFF FEAR

of drawing more intimacy and bringing us back towards a heart of worship together.

As we get out from among the four walls of a congregation and look passed our differences, and learn to become one body that truly loves God and each other despite our denominational differences. We are then able to peer into His full embodiment, as He always intended to bring us all to His love and make us one with His Father and the full Trinity. Can this still happen in a congregation or church building? Absolutely, and we are part of a great one, but it also helps to embrace the act of loving well and bringing Christ to those who may not always feel comfortable coming into a church building due to the differences in how we view simple doctrinal teachings. After all, we do not want to miss out on being able to share our King with everyone, including those who just need to be loved where they are, in their own places. So, the idea of how we view church just needs to be enlarged as we draw people to our homes and open ourselves to love our neighbors and those He may be sending us regularly in our workplaces.

The Diamond in the Rough—The Fire in the Pressing

After the prophet, let's call her Dee, ministered from the Word. She gave the opportunity to every woman to share their heart and needs for prayer. I felt safe and invited into their already-formed intimacy, and it opened the doors for a prophetic word that began to shift things for me. She declared that God had good changes up ahead for my growth and much mentoring was coming this next season. They prayed for healing over my heart from past hurts, and that spring boarded me into a great love encounter with God. I felt completely blessed by the love that these women had shown me, and thus I took them up on their later invitation to come out to another conference.

The next conference, held on October 26–27, 2018, was yet another setup by the Lord, called "The Time of Refreshing." Have you ever walked into a room that was completely different than you expected? The freedom was very apparent as there was dancing with prophetic flags, and intense and artistic expression radiated through the corridors as people walked around with joyful arms outstretched towards the Lord. The speakers were diverse in gifting and denominations. There was a priest who stood up and gave a portion of the lesson, as this was a catholic sanctuary open for all denominations to come freely, and the spirit moved upon every individual that shared. I witnessed a full table set before us that had beautiful food being prepared and served. A few prophets were present and shared from a place of complete abandonment. It was amazing as they called us up at one point to prophecy through spontaneous worship. A few of us stood in a lineup, preparing our hearts to sing before a congregation. Despite my inability to have any rhythm or melody, I just turned off the worldly expectation and turned on my spiritual ear, I asked the Lord for a heavenly melody, and for the first time ever, I began to sing a prophetic melody with much joy and blessing. God's power moved through me and unto many others. It was a great JOY!

Have you ever let go and let God, despite your shortcoming? Have you taken steps forward to trust His full presence to meet you where you are at? It is not an easy task to say, "God, I believe you can use me in this manner to teach or to minister, even if I don't know what I am doing. It's your Spirit that will lead me when the going gets tough." I knew at that very moment that this was a place of complete reliance upon Him. It was in that moment that I experienced a great breakthrough. It was His moving and His spirit coming to rescue me. He began to give me a psalm and joy to deliver His song in a way that made people smile. It was beautiful, joyful, and for me, life-changing.

After we ministered, we were asked to stay in the front as the prophetic team walked around to pray for each of us. As they ministered, I felt God's hand come upon my heart. It was profound. It was at that moment, for the first time, that I met a stealth prophet who walked towards me and began to pour out what appeared to be buckets of imaginary joy barrels over my head. I was seriously confused as it was not a normal occurrence. So, I walked away and tried my best to stay away from this very mysterious messenger until he found me and walked to my aisle, and as he came to my seat, he handed me a folded note. I took it into my hands and began to open this little paper. It clearly read, "Next Level, POWER UP!"

After reading these words for the first time, shockwaves began to pulse through my entire body. I jolted straight into my chair and began to feel electricity charge into my whole body for what felt like twenty minutes. I shouted as waves of God's power surged through my limbs, I thought I was going to be chargrilled, but he had mercy and just wanted to unearth the dead branches and bring forth the attention of my heart. I knew that the Holy Spirit had changed me. As I came up from this intense presence, my friends who traveled with me kept saying look at your neck and face and arms. I stared at my hands because there was speckled dust of what appeared to be gems shining from my skin. It was not golden like most appearances, but it was like diamond dust that just covered me from head to toe.

The next day of this conference, the words and messages shared by the prophet were spectacular as he described the story of Elijah and Elisha. He spoke about it being a season of a double portion anointing. I believe that this is a pressing time for us to begin to see the gold and diamonds in our lives brought to the surface, and every gift that God has placed inside of us is waiting to be activated so that His kingdom can start to shine in all brilliance, through His sons and daughters. When Elijah approaches Elisha in 1 Kings 19, it's so radical when listening to their first encounter with each other. Elisha was plowing his fields with his twelve oxen, and Elijah walked over and threw his mantle over his body. When he did this, it became a similar call to one that Jesus gave His disciples, "Follow me!" What power and authority were being carried, that Elisha immediately just stopped what he was doing, went back just to kill his oxen and give away his tools as he knew he would never need them again, but chose to follow God's way instead. Though he was called and chosen, it still required a sacrifice on his part. It will take work to stay on that path and to keep trusting when everything around you seems to say to turn back and stop advancing.

In times of unsettling circumstances, discouragement may try to creep in, as it did with Elisha. His whole devoted time had been pressed towards serving Elijah, but as the time neared for him to be called up and taken away from him, he knew that it was then that he had to hold on tighter to gain the prize. Many times, he was told by his mentor, "Stay here while I go." However, Elisha knew that there was a pressing through that would keep him close and not allow him to grow lukewarm, watching from a distance as the action happened. No, he was ready to pay with his whole life just to be right there with his feet marking the frontlines. If we will press into God during the harder-dark moments and allow His pruning shears to trim our wicks until they are pressed and ready, we will also benefit from the reward that comes in the morning as his son rises upon our land and nation.

Elisha held on up to the very moment that his teacher was taken up in a whirlwind as chariots of fire swung him up into the air. All Elisha could do was watch as it all happened right next to him. But as he kept his eye single, he was able to witness the mantle falling and the transfer of God's anointing being released over his life in a double portion measure as he had dared to ask and believe more of God. Then as he pulled the mantle up, he took it and struck the Jordan River and parted the water so that he could pass. Open eyes watched from all around as they understood that a new power had just been released. What a sight that must have been, what a new sound that garment made as it split the waters in two and told the world a new victory awaits as you walk on through. Greater measures are in store for those who will contend for more to be released with such violence that they won't let go until it is manifested in their lives and into all things around them.

I left so changed by this meeting; my heart was burning with His fire. I remember driving my friend home, who had been traveling with me for quite some time as she did not have her own set of wheels, and the Lord spoke to me and said, give her your car. I thought for a moment and then spoke in my heart to the Lord, let me just check with my husband as we are one. So, as I announced to him the next day that we had to give our car away, he listened and prayed and then concluded that three vehicles were far too much for us anyway. That began a new ministry. We gave our vehicle away and allowed God's love to grow us in a much deeper selfless way, which became the first of a couple of vehicles we would give later. And for an entire year, we kept seeing sprinkles of diamond dust come upon our hands in the morning, day and night, as evidence that he was bringing us into His holy consecration. Even our children began to be sprinkled with dustings of the Lord's glory as a sign. We would say to them, "Look at the glory dust of God that's coming from the inside out, to say I'm in you carving out the diamond in the rough." It became a time of just marveling at how connected we are to His presence and how eager He is to show up in greater ways for our whole family and lead into our nation.

Our command is not to seek Him through signs and wonders, but He does promise that signs and wonders will follow them that believe. Our command is found in Matthew 28:18–20 (NKJV):

> And Jesus came and spoke to them, saying, "All authority has been given to Me in heaven and on earth. Go therefore and make disciples of all the nations, baptizing them in the name of the Father and of the Son and of the Holy Spirit, teaching them to observe all things that I have commanded you; and lo, I am with you always, even to the end of the age." Amen.

Prayer for Our Gifts to Be Chiseled Out

Father God, we thank You for transformation as Your fullest measure of heat is being poured into our lives. We are laying our lives into a pressing block before You and allowing Your stone to roll over and through us so that we can be processed into the finest and purest olive oil. We want to be refined so that everything that remains standing in us will be the grain of the best choice. We do not want to allow any mixture with the world to lead us away or draw us into complacency.

Father, I ask You to release the yoke of fear from the lives of Your children. Lord, sweep into the hearts of everyone that seeks You first and bring healing from the torments of fear. Thank You for sending Jesus to destroy the works of the devil and to release life abundantly! He who sins is of the devil, for the devil has sinned from the beginning. "For this purpose, the Son of God was manifested, that He might destroy the works of the devil" (1 John 3:8, NKJV).

As we partake of Your love, may abundant life become an avenue of growth over our lives. That we may reproduce fruit that is after Your kindness, patience, peace, and love. Help us to look into the mirror of Your Word and allow washing to come over our minds and our souls so that we can be restored to new abundant life. Release the oil of your grace over the hearts of your children and nation. Remove the heavy cloud of remorse and break open the brass heavens to bring such unity back to Your sons and daughters. In Jesus' name. Amen.

- CHAPTER 5 -

FOUR SCROLLS FROM THE BOOK OF ESTHER

In recent times, during my worship with the Lord, I began to receive visions of heaven, and specific scrolls started to be unlocked. As I rested under His glory cloud, I began to see the brightness of the Lord's light. A magnification of His glory opened my spiritual eyes. Intense flashes of light flickered, and I perceived images as you would see in a power point, only they were driven by circuits of flashes and energy. Every image was being engrafted from heaven. I was starting to see images of areas that looked like vaults. The dials of the vault were turning, as I saw mechanical cogs being turned by angels, and many turned in different directions, as each was leading into an opening of doors. I remember shouting out loud, "Doors upon doors are being opened!" I could see the angels of the Lord quickly rushing into the vaults and carrying the scrolls with them. They looked and spoke with their eyes and began to say, "These scrolls from the book of Esther are now being released unto the earth." It dawned on me that more revelation of the times and seasons was being handed to the sons for deeper understanding. I watched as these scrolls were launched into the earth, and in great excitement, I began to shout again, with an unhindered shout of triumph, "The destiny scrolls from the book of Esther are being released!"

What did this all mean? I couldn't help but remember the scripture in Esther, which we all hear time and time again, the phrase Mordecai used to let Esther know that if she did not rise, there might be another that would be risen in her place to redeem the Israelites, "Who knows if perhaps you were born for such a time as this." It's a very timely reference and had to do much with the channels and gears which I saw through the spiritual lens of time. I believe that God is giving us a window in time where we can begin to help steward His plans over the heart of our nation if we will follow His leading and lean into His instructions found in His Word, as well as come into alignment through submission. The following four areas were what I heard God say He was getting ready to do upon our nation. First, He has released a time for purification and identity restoration, a time to be cleansed with His holy fire to step into the new ground (new wineskin). Second, He is showing us the time and season we are living in and giving us an awareness of our purpose and plans so that we may place our hands on the plow and begin to reap from the fields which are ripe and ready for a grand harvest. Third, He is taking away the fear and reproach of the little lions and filling us up with His boldness and reverence of the Lion of Judah as He anoints us to seize the time. Lastly, He is teaching us how to legislate from a place of authority in the King's court, leading to a movement of changes all around our nation and unto nations of the world. This will be a key to effective, fervent prayers that will help us impact circumstances and events in each environment he lays before us at this time. As we learn to take our places, there will be territory taken back as the kingdom of God continues to be revealed across the nations of the world.

A Time of Cleansing (Consecration Fire) - Purity and Preparation "Esther"

When we look closer at Esther, it's important not to go through the chapters quickly but to ponder on every dynamic representation and symbol that reflect the trinity and the preparation of the spotless bride as there are nuggets of gold waiting to be discovered. When our Lord Jesus Christ returns, He is looking for a bride that is without spot and wrinkle (Ephesians 5:27).

During his reign, King Ahasuerus ruled over 127 providences and sat in the palace in the city of Susa, the capital of Persia. At this time, his influence and power had grown substantially. We can see this in the elaborate celebration and feasting that he had for seven days, with much wine and gifts given to many leaders of the provinces. On the seventh day, however, when he was merry after much wine, he called for Queen Vashti to appear before him and his leaders. However, her resistance and defiance brought rage over the King, as her disobedience had impacted his image before his leaders. Thus, they recommended that he remove her from her place as queen and install one who was more worthy of the title than she was. Though the King obviously enjoyed her company, he could not let her go unpunished, as many leaders feared that if an example wasn't made of her disobedience, many wives would adopt the same behavior and stop listening to their husbands or submitting to their leadership or authority.

So, the removal of Queen Vashti in Chapter One can be represented as the outcome that will come to those who do not respond to the king's invitation or take it seriously. Queen Vashti had much beauty and vanity; however, her position had caused her to become complacent. She thought she could do as she pleased with no regard to the crown, or perhaps she just despised having to parade her beauty before every male that thought of her as another object. Her displeasure is not fully known, except that she was willing to dismiss this request and defy these orders at the highest cost; unfortunately, this led to her abolishment away from the king's presence and into an unfinished ending.

If we were to compare this lesson to the church body, we have had churches in positions of leadership that have become complacent and do not honor the King's request to shine His glory. Their agendas have become influenced by world systems and replaced by lukewarm standards, and their vanity has become more important in the race to have more members than to win more souls into salvation. Their sinful motives lead many to darkness, and because they have not been called out, they have no fear of being exposed by agendas that do not lead to righteousness. In the Word, we are reminded that pride comes before a fall. In this same manner, many leaders have forgotten to honor God in many areas of their lives, thinking that it is their hard work and dedication that got them into their placement. This is the hour and time when an outpouring of the Spirit of God is moving to release Godly reverence through the church and nation. God is looking for leaders that will re-establish His ways and bring honor to His kingdom.

Humility—Losing Our Lives to Gain His Heart

We see that the king was served by seven eunuchs and received advice from seven princes equaling 7x7. When I looked that up in the biblical sense, I gathered the following info from a Bible study for the meaning of numbers; The total number of originally inspired books was forty-nine, or 7x7, demonstrating the absolute perfection of the Word of God.[7] The Bible holds the truth of the completeness of God. I also see a symbolism of how the Holy Spirit is reflected in seven lampstands and is known as our great counselor who leads us to find the answers we may need when it comes to affairs of the kingdom. Every good king should have wise advisors. Even Esther, in the second chapter, is given seven maidservants to tend to her needs, symbolizing a time of preparation by the seven spirits of the Lord. As I sought the Lord for its representation, I also heard the length of days for full creation to take place and enter His rest. The seventh day was such a blessing and was created so that we could take our time and be present with the Lord after all our work was complete. Much of our preparation work can be seen in our union with Christ, as He already did all the work so that we can learn what it's like to rest in Him.

In Chapter 2, verse 3 of the book of Esther, the king appointed agents in each province to bring these beautiful young women into the royal harem at the fortress of Susa. Hegai, the king's eunuch in charge of the harem, will see that they are all given beauty treatments. The representation of the eunuch, Hegai, can be seen as a representation of one who is our helper, who is assigned to help us here on earth with the task of our preparations for our union with our King. Yes, we can ask the Holy Spirit for help in preparing us to be cleansed and prepared for our precious Lord's return. After all, He is so pleased to present Jesus to us and through us.

In John 15:26 (ESV), it states:

> But when the Helper comes, whom I shall send to you from the Father, the Spirit of truth who proceeds from the Father, He will testify of Me.

Also, John 16:7 (ESV):

> Nevertheless I tell you the truth. It is to your advantage that I go away; for if I do not go away, the Helper will not come to you; but if I depart, I will send Him to you.

As we submit to the Lord's process for our lives, we too can find favor, as Esther did, first with Hegai, then leading to the king. We must submit our own will and ready ourselves with oil in our lamps as the five virgins did. The oil, in this case, can represent more of the Holy Spirit's preparations for our lives. It could also be symbolic of our callings and the usage of our gifts. As we keep serving and loving others well, we are obtaining more oil. Let us not be found without oil as the time draws near for our beloved's return. In this case, it describes that all ten virgins slept while they waited for their bridegroom until a voice went out at midnight, and they heard their beloved was coming. As they arose and trimmed their lamps, the five wise virgins had oil in their lamp, and the other five realized they had no oil left. In their attempt to make it to see their groom, they had to return to buy oil and were left behind. The wise virgins entered the door and were reunited with their bridegroom (Matthew 25). In this same likeness, those oil-filled lamps must be continuously receiving the nectar of His love and marinating under His presence.

Chapter 2, verse 4 describes that after the preparations, the young woman who most pleases the king would be made queen. This advice was very appealing to the king. Thus, he put the plan into effect. How wonderful it would be to please the King! In Genesis 5 (NLT), we hear of Enoch, who went to be with God without seeing death because he pleased God and "walked with him so closely." What a brilliant relationship he had obtained, enough so that God could not wait for him to be taken back home so he could be completely united. The prayer of my heart has been a steady one, regularly asking God to help me have faith that would please Him and worship that would draw me ever so near to Him. That I would disappear into His likeness by a transfiguration of becoming just as He is. This all can only happen by a postured heart of humility before our King of Kings.

In some engagements, there is a measure of time for preparation that takes place before the wedding date comes. Do you remember preparing for an event (such as a wedding)? Did it take you a long time? What did that preparation feel like to you? Were you excited? In our experience, we had courted for three years and knew that God was calling us into the union. Our wedding was overlooking the mountain tops of Tehachapi, California, on the ridge of our pastor's backyard.

Despite the lack of time and preparations, it was still the most beautiful wedding ever, as it had all the right settings, sunshine glistening over colorful ridges which had hawks flying over the sunset skies, friends who had become like family and family who supported and loved us dearly. The grace we felt was a foretaste of God's favor on that day, leading to many more that would increase as we drew closer to him together. Esther did not have the luxury to choose how she would prepare as it was already chosen for her. However, she did submit her life to God and allowed her name and past to be forgotten so that her future could be reshaped and formed.

We are told very little about Esther's preparation except the following: In Chapter Two, verse twelve, before each young woman was taken to the king's bed, she was given the prescribed twelve months of beauty treatments—six months with oil of myrrh, followed by six months with special perfumes and ointments. The number twelve is the governmental number meaning perfection. It is also the product of three, which signifies divine, and four, which signifies earthly. It was twelve chosen disciples who witnessed the acts of Jesus on this earth and learned as His students. Twelve can be found in 187 places in God's Word, twenty-two times in Revelation alone. It's the number of the sons of Israel, and it's the number of the New Jerusalem with its twelve gates, which represent completeness, wholeness, and so much more.[8] I am sure you can think of more that I may not have mentioned. However, as we look at number interpretation, it is imperative that we only interpret these numbers by the leading and prompting of the Holy Spirit to view them from His biblical state.

As we look at the oils that were prescribed, we know that she was to be in oil of myrrh for six months. We also see Myrrh as it was presented to Jesus at His birth. I believe this was a symbol of His life's cause, representing one who was kept perfect and pure and would cleanse the sins of the world (Matthew 2:11, frankincense, myrrh, and gold).

I always envision this part as Esther steps into the process and submits her way. She walks into a journey of metamorphosis. In similarities to Jesus, he gave up a life in heaven to come down and reshape our inheritance. Where her past identity was being restored into a new identity, and she was obtaining what Jesus came to give. The one year would be a deep spiritual encounter and awakening, one of renewal. She would go from being a caterpillar of noble lineage and transfigure into a woman of valor and royalty as her inheritance with beautiful wings to set flight!

In my research on myrrh, it is believed to have medicinal properties, such as anti-aging, preventing wrinkles, helping with hormonal, stimulating circulation, decreasing inflammation, soothing inflamed skin, healing fungal infections, alleviating stretch marks, and repelling insects and parasites.[9] Thus, the first six months were used for cleansing and purification. Let's look at this from a spiritual context. What are some ways we become purified in our souls? As the bride, we are called to be cleansed by the blood and washed by the Word of God in our lives. We allow the Lord to heal our wounds, and our soul is made excellent again. We can look at myrrh as a physical representation of spiritual light per se, as where there is light, there can be no darkness. And we can see Jesus as the light (word) who came to bring us to Himself. That Word cleanses our hearts and allows us to be made complete, lacking nothing. In Psalm 51:7 (NLT):" A prayer from King David, after he was confronted by Nathan about having committed adultery with Bathsheba. Purify me from my sins, and I will be clean; wash me, and I will be whiter than snow."

Once they were certain she was free of disease or any fungus, they spent the next six months accentuating her outward beauty. In the spiritual realm, beauty treatments can be seen as an illuminating of her gifting and joy coming forth to shine her inheritance from the inside out, a showcase of the Lord's glory over her life. So, the additional six months were time spent on spices and cosmetics, making her radiant. We do not know the exact things they used, but if we look at some of the spices being used in that region of the world, we could consider Frankincense as part of a product to make the list. Frankincense has a sweet aroma and is highly used as a cosmetic, including the production of Kohl, which is evidently seen in ancient Egyptian art, a depiction or imagery found on many hieroglyphs, "sacred carvings," found on temple walls.[10]

As Jesus "Christ" or "Messiah" means "one who has been anointed." The significance of the anointing oil used over Esther can be seen as a representation to draw us closer to Jesus through this symbolic anointing of coming into one with Christ. We begin to receive His revelation and beautiful oils for healing and for miracles as we marinate in His presence and promises. Oils of gladness fall upon our heads as we learn to forgive and live in all His freedom. Our prayers can then become a fragrance before God's throne as He views us through the lens of His beloved Son, with who we are completely united as we are submerged in His oil. At the end of the preparation, we are adorned with His garment and become His beloved bride! When Esther's time arrived, she was allowed to take anything to wear and chose only what was recommended to her by the eunuch Hegai, she then continued to find favor with everyone, including the king himself.

In Chapter 2, verses 16–17 (NIV):

> She was taken to King Xerxes in the royal palace in the tenth month, the month of Tebeth, in the seventh year of his reign. Now the king was attracted to Esther more than to any of the other women, and she won his favor and approval more than any of the other virgins. So he set a royal crown on her head and made her queen instead of Vashti.

We come to read that with gladness, the King placed the royal crown upon her head and made her queen in place of Vashti. Another symbol of the seventh can be seen in the years of the king's reign, perhaps symbolism of a time she entered rest. Finally, we are crowned with His signature love. We are united into a place of royalty with the King of our hearts. This is the time we have been waiting for. The most wonderful union brings about immeasurable glory upon this Earth.

It's all about humbling ourselves and allowing Jesus to place His radiance over our hearts and change our lives to be one with Him! Marriage to the lamb does not need to be something we wait for until He returns. It can be a receiving of Him in this very moment as the

Father reveals to us His fullest love and grants us access to all His inheritance in the now. Your promise of being fully taken up can be seen in the likeness of the new wine miracle. Though it was not quite time yet, Jesus's mother knew that the promise He held could reach outside time due to His goodness. Thus, in her glimpse, she saw it already happening. Her faith touched new ground (John 2:1–11). Yes, He is coming back again, and we are excited about that day. However, until that time comes, we must occupy every area He places us in.

A Sense of Time (To Complete Our Mandate Upon This Earth)

As the darkness grows, we know that there is simply a need for the light to shine brighter. In Chapter 3 of Esther, we read about the position of elevation given over to Haman. He seemed to be one who would take the credit for another man's accomplishments. Though Mordecai had uncovered a conspiracy against the King and kept them from succeeding, he was not acknowledged, but instead, another was elevated ahead of him. And simply because Mordecai refused to bend a knee to this leader, there was a seed of offense that grew. Leading to an attempt to destroy an entire nation. What pride looks like as it edges its way into the heart of man, one becomes so blind to think that they could rise ahead of the Lord's called and chosen. And as the Bible speaks clearly in Proverbs 16:18 (NKJV): "Pride goes before destruction, And a haughty spirit before a fall."

After Queen Esther heard of the oppression that now lay upon her nation as evil plans had been arranged by Haman to eliminate and annihilate her people, she was given an ultimatum. Through the wisdom of Mordecai, he presented an option that called Esther into proper alignment. Through prayer and fasting, she would seek God for divine favor and then step out in faith. She was to consider approaching the King in hopes of exposing the gruesome plans laid out by Haman. Would she be able to stop him before they could be carried out? She knew that if she went into the King's presence without an invitation, he could simply have her killed, and apparently, his reputation of being vicious preceded him on many accounts.

Esther began a three-day national fast, asking God in prayer to grant her and her people access to His divine favor. She knew that those who find favor with God should surely be granted favor with man as well. Could you imagine what went through her thoughts those three days, as she knew that her life and the life of her people depended upon her obedience and access to God's wisdom in that moment? The Bible speaks much about fasting, and in so many ways, it should become such an intricate part of our lives. But to come together as a nation and humble ourselves takes the leading of the Lord, impressing upon strong men and woman to be made lowly, with intentional heart pursuit, just as found in 1 Kings 21:27–29. As she was applying fasting to help to seek God's guidance, similarly found in Judges 20:26. She also sought deliverance and protection for her life and her people like 2 Chronicles 20:3–4. And, of course, like Ezra 8:23, Esther wanted to strengthen prayer and have clear soundness before she went before the king.

Many have come to points of seeing their lives at a major crossroads and have been asked to take their hands off the wheel and seek God earnestly while He could still be found. It may be that at this very moment in time, the whole heart of our nation is waiting for us to come before our God in prayer and fasting to receive His impartation of favor and peace to carry out His purposes instead of allowing the evil plans to take root. We should not move until we have sought the Lord first. As we learn that He is waiting to release more of His blessings if we will just come into a place of shedding off the excess and lose our agendas so that we may come into His presence. It is these moments that will propel us into taking action that will be covered by His favor.

Remembering back to 2013, when I was having some devotion time with God. He began to speak very clearly over my heart, and He placed an idea or thought over my mind. Would you have accomplished everything I sent you to do if I took you out of this Earth by the end of this year? I immediately began to ask a lot of questions like, "God, do I only have a year to live? What am I doing right now that is bringing honor to your kingdom?" He lovingly reassured me through peace that He just wanted me to measure my time and energy to have it be effective in doing the things that mattered most. It was during that time that I took account of all my endeavors up to that point and began to write and blog about everything He had been saying. I started a web challenge called Project 365—A Step Closer to Jesus. I began to document our journey of ideas and concepts as well as the next steps that would draw our family into the nearness of being next to our Father daily. Somehow, my husband and I knew that it required a postured heart that would lean into Him on every level. It's these moments incorporated into our life's journal that has allowed me to see the progression that has been steadily leading us into a deep trust as we have spent time seeking and searching Him out. He promises in His Word that those who seek with all their hearts will find Him. Jeremiah 29:13 (NIV):

> You will seek me and find me, when you seek me with all your heart.

Perhaps, in similar ways, I could relate to Esther as her trust had been already stretched, and now, she had come to the end of herself. She came back to a place of knowing that her God was much bigger and offered a much greater inheritance outside of just this life on Earth. Esther was ready to give it all up, at the cost of saving her people, in her lifetime. No amount of schooling could have led her to make such a mature decision. It had to be an impartation of divine exchange. As she prayed and fasted, the Lord moved everything into its proper way and order so she could enter His favor. It was there all along. She needed only to uncover and grab hold of it! The realm of the Spirit became an open corridor that would help her face anything, even the end of her own story. A time to unlock the greatest part of His story, the revelation that the King of Kings is gracious and worth everything; giving up our lives is only the beginning of a setup into a step-up (Christ's revelation).

Removal of Fear and Reproach (Time of Boldness)

On the third day, Christ arose from the grave and released every captive into eternal salvation. Fear lost its grip over the hearts of man! A holy boldness came over the disciples as they received word of the Lord and His resurrection. What a stirring their hearts must have felt! Knowing that the one they had vowed their hearts to was truly the Messiah, who had come to take away the sins of the world. The removal of our sinful nature is now severed off, and we do not have to continue in a false covenant, but instead, we are to be bonded with Jesus daily and allow His righteousness to adorn us as a new garment. His goodness is being poured out and wants to be displayed through the lives of His children. Will we step into the blessings which our Father intended for us? It's time to stop expecting the worst! Our God is a good and merciful Father who loves us dearly. He watches His children and protects them from the assignment of the evil one. He hedges us into the palm of His hand and sets His angels around us to keep us from falling into the traps of the enemy.

As we read Esther chapter five, we hear about how on the third day, Esther placed her royal gown and attire as she made her way into the royal court. Could you imagine what was going through her mind as her heart raced as she took what could have been her last steps? She was adorned in splendor, and a holy boldness moved her forward. When the king saw her, she immediately found favor in his sight as he extended the royal scepter in his hand toward Esther. As she approached the king, she touched the tip of the scepter. As the king inquired what her request was, he was willing to give her up to half his kingdom. She is bold in her request as she asks the king to bring Haman with him to a banquet that she has prepared. Gleefully, the king rushes to meet this request. This is the time for Esther to arise with boldness.

As they meet the next day for an eloquent picnic with the queen, they enjoy the delicate food and lush wines. In a time of being merry, the king asks Esther, "What is your request?" Again, the words, even up to half my kingdom, will be fulfilled. The Lord directs Queen Esther in her handling of this important petition as she playfully gives way to building her king's patience. Perhaps, it's to build intrigue over the heart of a king who was so used to getting everything when he demanded. She leans in and requests that both the king and Haman come to another banquet the next day in hopes that the next day will be her moment of truth. This pleases the king as he grants her request. Haman, on the other end, is sent home, boasting of his position and recognition before the king and his queen.

At the banquet hall, they meet for the second time with Queen Esther. This time, she exposes the plot of her enemy Haman, who had planned all along to destroy and annihilate her people. The plot of wickedness carried by Haman is exposed right in his face, and as he pleads for his life, it is seen as a threat to Esther. The king calls for Haman to be hung on the same gallows which he had built that same day to have Mordecai hung. Thus, turning the circumstance around for the Jews. God always has a greater plan; we hear this in Genesis 50:20 (NKJV):

> But as for you, you meant evil against me; but God meant
> it for good, to bring it about as it is this day, to save many
> people alive.

Esther's quick response in seeking God first empowered her into boldness, propelling her before the king and changing the course of her nation. The original intent of destruction was defused, and a new plan to restore her nation came as she exercised her place of authority and power. What will you do with your giftings and placement during this time of great significance?

There have been many plots determined for our nation, and in some cases, judgment is still swinging the pendulum to the left, echoing emerging destructions. Considering the impending words, my heart seeks that which the Lord desires to bring about a restoration over a land that is willing and able to come into humility. Just as we read in history, when a nation has turned from its wicked ways, many have been spared from the grips of terror and death. As hearts were repentant and submitted just as those described in 2 Chronicles 7:14 (NIV):

> If my people, who are called by my name, will humble
> themselves and pray and seek my face and turn from their
> wicked ways, then I will hear from heaven, and I will
> forgive their sin and will heal their land.

Legislating Prayers of Authority (A Time for Leaders to Arise)

As Esther's favor is restored with the king, she and Mordecai must stop the plans and learn to legislate from a higher realm of faith. They receive great wisdom from the Lord and begin to re-write a new law and edict. They returned the confidence back to the Jewish people and gave them orders to protect and war against their enemies. Much can be done when hope is restored. Having the signet ring of the king changed the course of the Jews' inheritance. And as many had seen the royal ascend of Mordecai into power, many in the land feared the Jews. The Jews were able to overthrow their enemies and take their places of authority back. As a National Day of Celebration on the fourteenth and fifteenth days of the month of Adar, it become a day of feasting called Purim. When the Jewish people celebrate their days of mourning, turning into days of great joy.

An example of authority being released in the word can be seen in Isaiah 22:22 (ASV):

> And the key to the house of David will I lay upon his shoulder; so he shall open, and none shall shut; and he shall shut, and none shall open.

This was the Spirit's commendation of the servant Eliakim, son of Hilkiah, who was honored due to his humility. This shows us how God sees the inner parts of a man's heart and motives and sets him over the affairs of a king's estate.

This similar phrase can later be heard as Jesus spoke over Simon and Peter in Matthew 16:13–20 (NKJV). As he had come into the revelation of knowing in his heart that Jesus was the Messiah, he spoke in response to being asked by Christ:

> "Who do they say I am"? Immediately Simon responds with a strong assurance could have sounded a bit like this, Of course, You're the Christ, the son of God. No other could do what you do. Immediately, Jesus turns to him and releases awareness that this was revelation given by Holy Spirit, as only he can bring this level of understanding. He then let him know that upon this Rock-solid principle shall come the establishment of his church. He also describes that the Keys are released over his house unto the disciples. And I tell you, you are Peter, and on this rock, I will build my church, and the gates of hell shall not prevail against it. I will give you the keys of the kingdom of heaven, and whatever you bind on earth shall be bound in heaven, and whatever you loose on earth shall be loosed in heaven." Then he strictly charged the disciples to tell no one that he was the Christ.

In similar ways, the keys of David's house gave Eliakim the authority to open and shut doors, and the keys of the kingdom gave the Apostles authority to bind and loose on Earth and in heaven. The great authority held by those who possessed the keys of the Good News of the kingdom requires wisdom in stewardship as through ministry, they release the power to save or to leave in condemnation all who hear the

Word. Thus, those who receive keys can open the door to the inner chamber of the King's house in order to provide an entrance for Israel and the nations.[11]

The Wonders of Our God

The Word of God is truth, it has life, and it is the source of instruction that we all need to grow in maturity with Christ! Out of the abundance of God's Word flows the oil of the Holy Spirit. I found this out one night as I was pleasantly shown. It was a living water monument that rose out of my word. What does this even mean? Well, let me explain. I was instructed by the Lord through His Spirit to meditate on the book of Daniel, it was late, and my husband was already asleep. As I began to read with a flashlight in anticipation, like a child who doesn't want to go to bed at the reading of her favorite story. I was in Chapter 7, and every time that I read verse 9, I watched as thrones were put in place and the Ancient One sat down to judge. His clothing was as white as snow, His hair like the purest wool. He sat on a fiery throne with wheels of blazing fire, and a river of fire was pouring out, flowing from His presence. Millions of angels ministered to Him; many millions stood to attend Him. Then the court began its session, and the books were opened (NLT). I closed my eyes and imagined this scene as it played out, and I noticed that the atmosphere around me was shifting. It felt supernaturally invigorating. I could see the Lord in all radiance as His hair was white and His throne was surrounded with fire. In that moment, I just felt like it became a reality. My senses were open to my

King, and every part of His kingdom was becoming a reflection at this moment.

In that place of awareness, I could hear the Holy Spirit's impression on my heart. As He spoke softly, I am pouring out my oil upon the lamp of your eyes. I felt so blessed by His touch, and then, as the light peered through the night darkness and uncovered pages of my Bible, I could see a drop of oil coming through my Bible. It began small and then grew to a smear and appeared as a smudge on the paper. I just held my light in focus and saw the oil continue to pour through the fabric of woven fibers. I knew I was witnessing a holy moment as God was communicating with me and wanted me not to miss this sign. Perhaps it was to show me that I had just touched a part of His holiness as I kept revering His beauty, as impressions of Him were pegged into my spiritual eyes.

I began to ponder on the details of the whole chapter, over and over, and I knew it all had to do with the authority that He had granted us to legislate in the courtrooms of heaven, where Jesus is our high priest. As it is in Chapter 7:14 (NKJV), He describes:

> Then to Him was given dominion and glory and a kingdom,
> That all peoples, nations, and languages should serve Him.
> His dominion is an everlasting dominion, Which shall not
> pass away, And His kingdom the one Which shall not be
> destroyed.

And the later parts of the chapter in verses 26 through 28, describe the decision that the court will pass in judgment, and all the powers of the evil one will be removed and taken away and destroyed. Wow, then the sovereignty, power, and greatness of all the kingdoms under heaven will be given to the holy people of the Highest. The final battle ends in great victory. The triumphant bride will inherit the Lord, Jesus, and live with Him for eternity. What great joy this vision brought me, both from the account Daniel had and then from the promises of God's grace through His oil pouring forth, which I believe was a great sign of blessing upon the time of harvest.

As our nation's soul is suspended upon a tightrope, the increase of satanic activity and spiritual assault has shown a progression against Christians. Making it a critical time to discern and come into agreement with the Word of God and faith. As God holds time, we step into Christ and push back against the antichrist agenda. If there is breath in us, we must keep speaking and standing for what is right and bringing about a shift in the existing rulings and decisions across our nation. It's by taking our places in this given hour. We need to arise and begin to shine. Every sphere of influence He has entrusted us with has got to be handled with care and precision. You heard me mention the seven mountains of influence. These areas need to become places we take ground back, as Joshua did in his later years. We have got to take the high ground and fight for what is ours. Three times Joshua was told by God, "Do not fear, have courage." He had to understand how much territory still needed to be occupied. It required his obedience and his strength in the Lord. We were not designed to be passive or called to just float on imaginative fuel. We were called to occupy this land. Our nation needs strong leadership that will represent the heart of the

Father. Leaders that will stand up and speak or stand up and build when the Lord says move. We are living in a day when the greatest miracles are ahead of us.

The question remains, are we willing to take our place in leadership among areas that we are called to impact? In our home, community, church, marketplace, business, education, music, and art, as well as every place of influence? The time is now, don't let another day pass over your vision for what God is asking you to step into today. Lead us into advanced territory, Lord.

- CHAPTER 6 -

CATCHING THE FIRE—
TORONTO, CANADA

Consecration Fire—The Process of Healing

We read and hear about the flames that surround the Lord's presence, but oftentimes we cannot just take small glimpses but peer into His heart and get so close that we catch embers and begin to burn with His love. After we become throne dwellers and let His love burn through our hearts, this is where the bluest flames of His revelation are made apparent to us. It becomes a place where God can make great exchanges with us: our hearts for His, our thoughts for His, and our distractions for heaven's focus and intent. It begins during our time with Him in the secret place, then moves wherever He sends us so that we will keep our flames ablaze and consume all things. As described by Patricia King in Elijah List in her article on October 17, 2006, she writes about, "The blue flame is the hottest and most intense part of a fire, and blue is often a prophetic symbol of divine revelation, God's love, and an open heaven."[12]

My husband and I came into a deeper burning as we sought the Lord through worship at specific times. The Lord then led us to certain places, as he called us to where the corporate revival was still happening. Two of those amazing events were both at the same location, just different years. In 2018, my husband and I attended the Light the Fire Again conference held in Toronto, Canada, sponsored by CFAN. The following year in 2019, we went back and again encountered God at His altar, where He was releasing a renewal of first love and a fire that was catching. It was such an amazing encounter, so I will share with you a few testimonies about the conference. It forever impacted our lives as we were brought into a deep consecration of His purest love, ignited by His flames of revival.

In April 2018, at the Light the Fire Again conference, my husband and I were in an open heaven after having spent four days under intense worship, word teachings, and impartations from the Holy Spirit. On the second day, God showed me His love in a new way. His sweet love was so tangible that I felt closer to Him than I had felt before. The next encounter was intense, as God began sharing His compassion for the lost, those who had died without receiving Him first. The tears poured down my eyes as I wept out loud for the entire afternoon. The Holy Spirit led me into deep mourning as I was shown the lake of fire carrying many who had not received Jesus! I was inconsolable, and at one point, my husband had to leave me there for a while as he went to gather lunch.

As the Lord ministered to my heart about how He sees the lost, it changed my heart completely, opening my senses to what it could be like for those who missed the mark prior to leaving Earth and didn't have to if only someone had shared the good news with them. For if they had known His goodness and His invitation, wouldn't they have chosen His life over theirs? This awareness strongly entered my heart as I realized that there is a time for us to run with the message of hope and life while there is still breath left in our lungs and in our brothers and sisters alike. This was the first time I had ever cried in such remorse as I connected to the Father's aching heart for them all as if He missed them in a way that caused His heart an excruciating pain as a piece of Him was being torn away. He had longed to be reunited with His beloved, and they had fallen short of just reaching out to His love. After coming to Earth and giving up His life for us to receive entrance into His heart, His blood was completely sufficient to meet every one of our needs. Sadly, if it was missed, it could have been because there was either no understanding of His love, rejection of His love, or no one had shared their story with the lost.

I believe that this is the hour that we should be praying for God to wake us up and shake us up, to bring us into an accounting and organization of our destiny scrolls so that we begin to become informed by heaven's time clock. Only then can our prayers ignited by faith begin to shift everything in our lives. We need to ask for our hearts, minds, and eyes to be opened by the Holy Spirit so that we are sensitive to working with the Lord and co-laboring with the angelic hosts that He has provided as helpers around us. These are the days we are called to be fortified with a foundational knowledge of our Father's love so that we can draw all men, women, and children back to the Father's original intentions. His heart does not desire that one should perish for the lack of knowledge. Hosea 4:6 (NKJV) states:

My people are destroyed for lack of knowledge. Because you have rejected knowledge, I also will reject you from being priest for Me; Because you have forgotten the law of your God, I also will forget your children.

During the third day of the Toronto revival, I was in deep worship. As the song was released by Roy Fields about His beautiful train filling the temple, I saw a vision of God's beautiful wind blowing the shiny luminescence of His train entering the sanctuary. It was purple and flowing with the wind of the Holy Spirit beneath it and over it. I saw in my vision that the royal purple cloth covered me from the beginning of my life to that very moment in time when I stood before Him and then all the way until the end of this lifetime! This train filling the temple is described in Isaiah 6:1–4. Its cover was unending, and it was glorious to be given an account of the longevity and protection over my life! I got a sense that I was receiving grace to endure my whole lifespan until the completion of my assignment from God, and for me, that was comforting. But in true reality, I realized that I would never truly be away from His presence.

I was being shown the grace under Jesus for my whole existence, that there was nowhere I could run that would take me away from His love. His love is always upon us, and He blankets us with His glorious presence, which becomes a robe of His glory! It is remarkable, and it never ends, as it keeps filling the temple repeatedly. Psalm 139:7–12 (NKJV) says:

"Where can I go from Your Spirit? Or where can I flee from Your presence? If I ascend into heaven, You are there; If I make my bed in hell, behold, You are there. If I take the wings of the morning, And dwell in the uttermost parts of the sea, Even there Your hand shall lead me, And Your right hand shall hold me. If I say, "Surely the darkness shall fall on me," Even the night shall be light about me; Indeed, the darkness shall not hide from You, But the night shines as the day; The darkness and the light are both alike to You.

His Kingdom in Us - A Vision

That same night of the conference, my husband and I were among the thousands that were prayed over during a fire tunnel led by the evangelist leading the others, and many anointed leaders walked around laying hands on the crowd. As they passed along and prayed, we both felt the Holy Spirit come upon us. As we both lay on the carpet, I had a magnificent open vision. I looked up and saw a blue altar of God open out of a blue mist, and I saw a slide come down like a shoot. I heard God's voice in my heart say, "What would you ask me for, daughter?" I thought for a bit and was in deep prayer for what I should ask for. I couldn't respond immediately as there was so much discussion happening in my mind, so the slide began to be rescinded back again. Then I felt a heaviness in my chest because I thought I may have missed the opportunity as I didn't ask quickly enough. However, under God's patience was His grace (and it sure was sufficient) as He surprised me and released a much bigger slide. It came closer to me, and I caught a view of the greatest treasure of all. I realized I was being shown the kingdom of heaven. It was brought from far away and appeared beautiful and amazing all together. My eyes lay hold of the kingdom, as a paradise, shone in all its brilliant light. I held it in my vision as it was brought closer. It got so near that my spiritual arms reached upward from within my womb and received it with my spirit arms (Holy Spirit in me). The kingdom was brought into my inner man!

The revelation God revealed was that He had paid such a high price for this present awareness that He wanted me to understand that we can have it all through Christ! It was so huge! It's even hard to describe, but it was our inheritance to receive His kingdom through Christ! I then fell into great laughter and rejoiced the entire night, giving God thanks for such an amazing revelation and gift! His kingdom was being revealed by having Christ within me, the hope of all GLORY! Yes, Christ is holding the revelation of the kingdom of God within His heart, and He chooses to reveal His Father and His kingdom to us, His betrothed bride. The kingdom of God is the realm where Jesus Christ reigns as King and Lord, and God's authority is supreme. This kingdom exists here and now in the lives and hearts of the redeemed, also in perfection and fullness as we look at the future when Christ returns.[13] He spoke clearly in Revelation that He was coming back soon. So, as we are excitedly awaiting our beloved return when He will wipe away every tear and rid this world of all darkness.

We can live in full communion by stepping into His authority and power and beginning the great work of taking back our land as Christ gave us the dominion to rule over the nations. Let's make sure that we do not take part in the "rapture rug fold-out committee," becoming passive and unattentively responding to the needs around us. Let us give God thanks for the bridge that Christ Jesus has made for us to receive our inheritance as kingdom dwellers. As He brought forth salvation by taking the place of our sins and became the final sacrifice so that we could enter His inheritance and His kingdom could become our resting place filled with His wisdom and peace. It is only by His great mercy that the revelation of heavenly treasures found in His heart can be transferred over to our hearts as we are truly one with Jesus. Hence, there could be a release of God's will and blessings upon this Earth, allowing His kingdom to manifest through His sons. Colossians 1:13–14 (NKJV):

> For he has rescued us from the dominion of darkness and brought us into the kingdom of the Son he loves, in whom we have redemption, the forgiveness of sins.

Asking God for the Nations

The final night, on day four of the conference, was a beautiful surprise. As the minister was speaking, she had the honor of the final scripture and message. She was very yielded to the Holy Spirit as she conveyed directly to our hearts about how many of us still don't have any clue who our Father truly is, as it is apparent in what we fail to ask for in our prayers. We kept asking for small things, like her children, who were rescued from much poverty, oppression, and abuse, and kept asking for beads to make a necklace, while God honored their request and sent them a blessing of beads. She wept at the fact that they could have asked for the nations but had settled because they had been oppressed long enough that they didn't know how much more was available to them. This can be evident in many people's lives when you hear their prayers. It's as if they have settled with not expecting much from God, and all the while, He is waiting on those that will pray dangerous, powerful prayers to release the blessing over entire nations and people groups.

She then spoke about the verse in 1 Kings 4:1–7. What was exciting was that on our way to Canada, my husband and I had been marveling at this scripture as a gateway revelation! We had been meditating on it with great emphasis. It was the scripture that God wanted us to rest on and believe Him to bear much fruit. In this story, Elisha is visited by a widow who owes lots of money, and her debtors are threatening to take her son. She pleaded for help, and Elisha asked her what she had in her home. She then tells him, "Nothing but a little oil." Elisha gives her instructions for multiplying that oil to pay her debt and thus, through her obedience, gives her even more to survive on! God showed me that as that woman moved in an act of obedience, I, too, was being asked to empty my vessels to receive so much more oil. God spoke to my heart. He said, "If you give Me everything, I will make the oils run through your life." He reassured me that the oil never stops flowing in our lives, for as long as we keep pouring out our gifts to help others pay off their debts, God will keep the oil freely flowing as there is plenty in the reserves of heaven!

As we come to a deeper understanding of who our Father is, we will stop asking Him for the little scraps and begin to ask Him for our true inheritance. We, as His church, should be standing on higher ground, desiring the nations as our inheritance. After all, He paid in full by the measure of His blood and life so that we could come into dominion on this Earth and bring His kingdom into manifestation through our faith and partnership with His Word. What has God been asking you to lay down before His altar? Many times, the things we have in our hands can be seen in a different light.

Sometimes, it just takes a moment to think outside the circle of your ordinary happenings and allow God to show you if there are existing areas in that He has given you influence. It may just require your obedient steps forward. God alone says ask of me, and you shall receive, in Matthew 7:7–8 (NKJV):

> Ask, and it will be given to you; seek, and you will find; knock, and it will be opened to you. For everyone who asks receives, and he who seeks finds, and to him who knocks it will be opened.

He also gives us insight from a higher perspective, a view from above, where the atmosphere is clear. As our reliance grows on hearing His voice, we can come to a point where we are doing all the things that matter most to Him, and it will reciprocate a great joy in us. As joy is a gift from our Father, He shows us the pleasure of revelation found in Christ's full victory in our lives.

Tarrying Until the Door Opens

The grand finale arrived as if things could get any more exquisite. After the final minister was finished, she gazed at the crowd of three thousand hungry radical Jesus followers, and she discerned that we had been fed well enough to now ready ourselves to enter His holy presence. Instead of doing the work for us, she challenged us all as she spoke in firmness and expressed that we all have been here for four days under the glory cloud. She spoke, "It's time church for us to learn how to begin pressing into His presence in a form of hunger and tarring as we ask the Lord to show up in greater power, friends. We are of a mature nature at this point." We received that challenge. As she walked off the stage to join us at the lower altar, we joined a chorus of thousands who cried out for more of Jesus in complete desperation. There was a firm unspoken truth that we all carried; we all were going to press in, even if it took us all night. It must have been about an hour long that we sang similar psalms that came from our hearts, one person would start, and then a swarm of hundreds leading to thousands would come into synchronization with that melody.

As some in the crowd began to get tired, I closed my eyes and had an open vision. I saw the young man next to me shouting with all his heart, "Don't get tired now, church. The Lord is coming!" His words were heard from afar and encouraged others to keep pressing.

Somehow, I knew that the young man was a pioneer in this age, chosen to lead a nation toward the heart of the Father. I joined him in this charge to bring about refresh and connect my spiritual eyes with what I longed so badly to see. My faith arose as I could sense that holiness was shifting. Jesus was nearing. It became a feeling of knowing that he was entering a corridor that led to the doorway, which would spring His river over us all. So, I, too, began to shout with a voice of authority, "He is right at the door. Keep pushing!" Our voices were being lifted higher, and they glided with ease upward into an already open heaven filled with His oil and ease. I could hear shouts from afar as if they were right near me.

The crowd began to press even more intensely until, to our wonderment, we all sensed that Jesus was truly opening a door, and we began to feel his rivers pouring among the altars and spreading over us all! First, as a heavenly flood as Jesus' presence graced us, I was wrapped by His garments, which wrapped me into His love. It would take another whole chapter to tell you of this encounter. It's as if Jesus swept in, riding on a river that was flowing with life. He wrapped me into His presence, then ministered for quite some time. I was speaking in tongues, and He was inviting me to speak with Him face to face. I kept asking Jesus to have His words written on the walls of my heart. Some of us were being flooded with His awakening like a marvelous river invigorating everything in its path. We became more awake, and the eyes of our hearts were flooding with so much light. His glory swept among us and moved over and through many of the three thousand hungry vessels, filling us all up to overflowing measures.

It was spectacular, something that I have yet to find the right words for, a place where heaven touched Earth and changed every one of us. At one point, I lost my members. Yes, my hands and feet had become just clinging limbs of wailing extremities as I yelled and shouted and laughed with great joy. I felt like God was answering Jesus' prayer as Jesus prayed in John 17:20–23 (NKJV) the following prayer:

> I do not pray for these alone, but also for those who will believe in Me through their word; that they all may be one, as You, Father, are in Me, and I in You; that they also may be one in Us, that the world may believe that You sent Me. And the glory which You gave Me I have given them, that they may be one just as We are one: I in them, and You in Me; that they may be made perfect in one, and that the world may know that You have sent Me, and have loved them as You have loved Me.

As the river of the Lord encircled us at the altar, an invitation was opened to pour out all my heart before His holy presence. Praying in tongues a million miles per hour seemed like the best way to tell Him everything, and as I spoke, I was not just giving Him my heart issues. There was also a download of His heart in exchange. It could have been days, hours, minutes, or seconds. All sense of time left me, and that's the only place I wanted to be forever. A perfect description of this is in Psalm 84:10 (ESV):

> For a day in your courts is better than a thousand elsewhere.
> I would rather be a doorkeeper in the house of my God than dwell in the tents of wickedness.

I was lost in Him when I felt someone tap the palm of my extended hands, which were held forward in a receiving position. They spoke into my ear loudly, "Receive the fire." My reaction was intrigue and surprise when I heard and felt it a second time, but as I looked up, there was nobody standing near me, just people fallen over and worshipping God. A lightning-like fire came over me at that moment, and a baptism at the altar by a blue fire that came down from heaven began. I will say His presence is more amazing than we can begin to imagine! What He has for us is so much more than we can envision! He encouraged me to start asking Him for more! So, I haven't stopped asking. I kept hearing there is so much more to be found in Jesus. As you are becoming one with Him, you shall start to receive the revelation of who you are, and your inheritance in Christ shall spring forth new life in immeasurable ways. Matthew 3:11–12 (NKJV):

> I indeed baptize you with water unto repentance, but He who is coming after me is mightier than I, whose sandals I am not worthy to carry. He will baptize you with the Holy Spirit and fire. His winnowing fan is in His hand, and He will thoroughly clean out His threshing floor, and gather His wheat into the barn, but He will burn up the chaff with unquenchable fire.

Cultivating the Fire-Revival Harvest Supernatural School (RHSS)

The fire entrusted to us must be cultivated through relationship and intimacy with the Father. I knew that this fire was not just for my own consecration. It was beginning to burn through my bones. In a way, I knew that everyone around me needed an awakening of this magnitude. It was one to be shared with the world. Too many times, I have watched people go to conferences and have radical experiences. However, over a period, they are back to the same conditions. Perhaps they did not always know how to cultivate this flame. This was not something that I was willing to lose in our lives. No, this was different. When we returned from Toronto, the opportunity presented itself to be part of a school of ministry that focused on the supernatural aspects of the kingdom of God. What that even meant, I had no clue. All I knew was that I was hungering after all that the Lord had for me. In September 2018, after reviewing an email that described the following areas of focus: Identity in Christ, the supernatural gifts, leading to activation in areas such as prophetic ministry, healing, and deliverance, and so much more. It really began to appeal to my heart. I knew that I needed to activate all the gifts God had placed inside of me. I could not bear to watch my talents just be buried in the ground any longer. Our family joined this school and sent me on a spiritual rocket ship that would mature me and lead me to my gifting.

In Matthew 25, we hear about the wicked servant who took the coins and hid them in the ground, as he was afraid that his master was a mean task master. The other two found ways to invest and produced more from the coins given to them. Thus, they received more coins as a reward. Eventually, the wicked servant was removed from his position by the master and was cast out into outer darkness. I longed to have my talents revealed and applied so that I would never have that same fear of not using them. There is also much more to be said about this scripture, as the very nature of knowing that our Father has our best in mind and heart allows us to never worry about failure under His grace. The tasks we are called into should be joyful, as our perception of God remains correct. He truly is a good Father and wants to help us in every way that we invite Him to help us.

It was a very big deal as it came with both a time and a financial commitment as well. I knew that we were a family on one income, which was going to be a challenge, but I also had seen God move in ways that I knew were powerful. His words became substance to my faith as I knew He could provide for this if it was His plan. I took time to pray and sought my husband's advice as I knew it was not just my decision to make, but instead, it was our whole family that was going to make this sacrifice. In about a week, my excitement grew even greater, and this time my desire was to press forward. Our family agreed it was a season for me to grow in all that the Lord had, and that door sprung wide open. This was a beautiful lesson in seeing how obedience is key to the Lord's provision. We read in 1 Samuel 15:22 (NKJV):

> Has the Lord as great delight in burnt offerings and sacrifices, as in obeying the voice of the Lord? Behold, to obey is better than sacrifice, and to heed than the fat of rams.

At first arrival at RHSS, the community of believers that were there was just as hungry as I was and shared my desire to be next to God always. They, too, had been seeking God for more, and the expectancy in this church was impregnated with the possibility of great and amazing outpourings of the Holy Spirit. For the first year, I was completely laid out and rolled out like a piece of clay, as my whole heart was transformed. Many times, I could be found on the altar of God, weeping in uncontrolled abandonment. It was in that place that I was healed of an orphan spirit, unforgiveness, and heartbreak. My past disappointments had prolonged their toll on my health, and the rolling depression that I regularly dealt with was being removed. I felt like God was adding back life on every level: physical, emotional, and spiritual. The Word was being taught in such a light, and the spirit of wisdom was removing every veil of uncertainty. All religious mindsets were being peeled back as I received the word of freedom. His sweet Spirit was bringing out levels of revelation that He wanted us to grasp. I also gave all rights over to Christ of the injustice done to me by those who had hurt me, either knowingly or unknowingly. It took me about a year to come into full forgiveness of all things suffered under other church leaders that had misunderstood my gifting because they did not understand what God was doing or the timing of things happening. Also, I had to forgive myself for all past missed steps. The Spirit of the Lord gives us the ability to forgive all transgressions and takes us to the point of perfect healing. This was the greatest breakthrough towards stepping into love and peace with the Lord and with man.

The pastors who are now apostles of the house, David and Tracy, were loving and accepting of us all. We came from so many different places. Some of us had previous experiences with God, while the rest of us had very little to go on. Either way, they loved us all the same and gave of themselves to teach us all that the Lord had given them. Their incredible love story touched so many around them. The selfless love that they walk in reflected God all around their body. In their own experiences, they had both come out of a life of hardship as they both were entangled in drugs and worldly dealings until both encountered God and were transformed into His likeness. Apostle David's testimony is powerful, as he gave his life to the Lord, then traveled to Brownsville in Florida, where he encountered the move of God that forever changed him and awakened him to be a mighty lover and follower of Christ. They did not just come out for themselves, but they came out and began a great journey of bringing many people out from places of addiction and into transformation. These amazing pastors would go into the streets and bring out people that did not know their value to instantly adopt them into the sonship of Christ's love. They began to open their home to the lost until, eventually, their homes were so full that God had to grant them more homes to house all the souls that He sent their way. Eventually, their house church became a larger gathering that needed a larger building. This was when God directed them to open a church. Today, God has blessed their ministry, Redemption House Life Center, tremendously, as they are also leading various ministries such as Missions for America, a food pantry to feed people across the Baltimore and Pasadena areas, RHSS, and hosting many events that continue to lead many to Christ.

The memory that forever edged into my heart is the washing of our feet as we were coming to the end of a semester. About forty of us remained after a full year, and we were invited to have our feet washed by our pastor after a teaching on servanthood. When He got to me, I still felt so unworthy as He looked up at me and spoke over me words that led to life. As He washed my feet, He encouraged me that the days of holding back and walking on eggshells were no longer in front of me. As the water turned into spiritual nourishment, the old dust of lies and confusion was being exposed and fully cleansed my whole being, all in Christ-perfect ways. As my feet were cleansed, so was the inner part of my vessel. I was redeemed from all forms of rejection that had begun so long ago, but on that beautiful day, my heart was free to be a daughter in full acceptance. So much freedom happened that day. It had been so long that I had been suppressing my love language to God, all due to the fear of man. Unfortunately, many are gripped with this fear and lack acceptance because they have been rejected most of their lives. God was telling me, through my pastor's kind actions, "You are accepted and loved here. We are your family!" He released an affirmation word that encouraged me: he spoke, "You become all that God has always intended you to be! Do not hold back!"

Why was this so impactful? Perhaps because I always felt resistance fighting against my destiny. For as long as I could remember, there was always something trying to dim my light. Perhaps I was trying not to look different from everyone around me, succumbing to the wallflower approach of trying to just fit in and belong, which had ultimately kept me from pioneering into new ground and becoming part of the new sound! As many people have asked me what was happening while I was at the alter most of the time, while in tears or in prophetic shouts, I would say, "It's like asking a butterfly what is going on inside your cocoon." Can you describe what happens when everything in you is being completely transformed and reawakened to new levels? I was most assuredly finding my identity in Christ all over again. He always knew where I was. I just didn't know how to come back to Him as in that first love encounter with Him.

The exterminator Jesus had begun deep work within our hearts and mind, ridding me of every lie and doubt which brought about fear, shame, and condemnation. As His Words began to cleanse our hearts, there was a washing away of religious mindsets. The kind that made us fear the unknown pathways that had not yet been revealed. As found in Isaiah 50:7 (NKJV):

> For the Lord GOD will help Me;
> Therefore I will not be disgraced;
> Therefore I have set My face like a flint,
> And I know that I will not be ashamed.

We began to meditate on His Words together and regularly on our own. It became the food for our nourishment and the life bread which set us into right standing. As we held the mirror of God's Word to our eyes and heart, we started to receive His light, and all truth entered in and replaced any hidden lies as well as agendas. When we allow God to enter our hearts, He can expose, then expel all lies and rejection. They must go! We are brought into relationship, and His deep love restores us to our rightful place in Christ. He alone can heal us of shame, guilt, or condemnation. Don't allow the enemy to infiltrate your lens. You must always keep love first. These were tremendous nuggets of wisdom gained while I took time to marinate in the grace of His presence.

For two more years, I would continue at the ministry school as I pressed the gas pedal forward and let the throttle accelerate. There was more maturing taking place as I read His Word and in exercising the spiritual gifts. The Lord added more oil to our lamps, and as we journeyed with Him, He showed us so many new aspects about Himself. Yes, it was like getting to know Him more every time we peered into His throne room. The more we saw and knew, the more we wanted to be near Him to keep obtaining His presence and goodness. His mercy was tilted towards us as we drew close to Him, and the incredible encounters that we had while at this school were out of this world. We became brothers and sisters who sought each other's best and looked out for one another, we prayed continually in the Spirit, and we worked together to draw others to know Him in similar ways. The pastors, evangelists, teachers, prophets, and apostles that were brought to us brought so much wisdom and insight as they each carried different giftings and provided opportunities for us to encounter God in similar ways. In their pursuit of Jesus, they had found entrant points through His Word and led us right into the most wonderful holy places with the King. They imparted so much of their oil and kept asking us to do the same. As we keep giving it out, it will be given back to us. The oil and fire will never go out for as long as there is an altar and a submitted vessel willing to burn for Christ. That was what our hearts were becoming, a living sacrifice to our Father.

Discipleship-Stepping into Good Mentor Relationships

As we come into growth in Christ, it is important to get into relationship with Jesus. He can bring us into a divine mentorship with His Spirit and Word. This is the first type of mentorship that is most effective and most evident, as the word itself has all the power to transform our entire lives. This blessing of having mentors found in the Word of God can be so plentiful and really can nourish us in any situation. Beginning with salvation and leading into full sanctification, which can all happen in one simple interaction with Christ. The second mentorship available is through men and women of God that are in our sphere of influence. Then as we keep growing, we can ask God if there are people whom we are to relate to that can help in our growth. He can then lead us to those who have a deep desire to see Him manifested in every area of their lives and ours as well. Having mentors who will disciple us is biblical, as we can see this evident through Christ's example as He led the twelve disciples to come into relationship with Him and unity with each other. Having strong mentors who will speak powerfully and give us insight along the way is imperative as we continue to grow into His likeness. It is wiser to receive from those who have gone ahead of us and have led us into existing paths through their pioneering accomplishments. After all, we are told in scripture that it is wisdom to learn from others' mistakes and not have to fall into those trenches due to our own failures if we remain teachable. Proverbs 1:5 (KJV): "A wise *man* will hear, and will increase learning; and a man of understanding shall attain unto wise counsels"; and Proverbs 9:9 (KJV): "Give *instruction* to a wise *man*, and he will be yet wiser: teach a just *man*, and he will increase in learning."

One of my favorite books, which I read long ago, was called *The Divine Mentor* by Wayne Cordeiro (Cordeiro 2007). In this book, he describes the best mentorship found in Christ through Holy Spirit and released in evidence through His Word. He beautifully lays out how our best mentors have been found within the pages of the word that we so highly value. As we truly learn how to come into relationship with God, He mediates so that we can enter deep mentorship by His Word, and the Spirit becomes the breath that leads us down the corridor of all scripture. It allows us to get the big picture that is meant to imprint upon our hearts. We are brought before heroes of the past who still echo their lessons obtained by every act of devotion to the Lord and every victory they acquired in faith as well as failures due to missed step they took, which caused hardships. I believe some of our strongest mentors can be those we can relate with the most at specific times in our lives. I know that at moments I related with King David, as I, too, was drawn by a psalmist's heart. I heard love songs toward King Jesus in my heart and would write them regularly. I knew that I was destined to rule and reign with Christ, but I was still learning how to trust and come into sonship through the book of Psalms. Then, at other times, I felt so close to Daniel, as I, too, found myself having dreams and visions that seemed to have so much symbolism. I knew that I could look at his blueprint to learn from his actions leading to his strong character. He was able to live during times that the world was so corrupt, yet he stood in so much strength and still carried a heart that was pure and wholesome toward the Lord. In Chapter 2 of *The Divine Mentor* book, the author talks about the school of Wisdom. In a section, he writes, "If consequences have a back-end price, Wisdom has a front-end price. It requires discipline, obedience, consistency, and above all else, time. Then it gladly pours on you it's promised tremendous riches." He goes on to describe the difference between consequence and wisdom, in that wisdom will teach you a lesson before you make a mistake. While a consequence allows you to make the mistake first, this is how you will come to learn the lesson. Wisdom puts a barrier at the top of the cliff to keep you from falling, while consequences will visit you in the hospital after you've had your injury (Cordeiro 2007). As evidenced through Solomon's teachings in Proverbs, it is much better for us to learn from the experiences of others than it is for us to make our own mistakes. However, we must be wise and discern how to walk between these two roads.

Another example of mentorship is a recent book more focused on discipleship. This book is called *The Lost Art of Discipleship, God's Model for Transforming the World* by Daniel T. Newton (Newton 2021). This is an amazing example of finding mentors that will help strengthen our walk with the Lord and lead us into true discipleship. There is so much powerful insight in this book, as it is a blueprint for our current church leaders to follow and step up during a time of learning to father our nation back into a place of restoration and healing. So many people need fathers, and this is a dynamic and impactful journey written by a leader who himself has learned how to disciple a young generation into the heart of the Father. As we say, "Do it again, God," we can ask the Lord to use us all in helping to become fathers and mothers as well as encouragers and humble ourselves to also be teachable to learn from those who are catching the fire and running with the Lord's pioneering spirit.

Honoring Relationships

As God sends us people whom He has chosen to be a part of our lives, it's so important to always honor and keep ourselves from becoming too familiar with these relationships. This familiarity could cause us to lose the blessing of new gifting or mantles that are being placed over those who we have walked with through long and difficult journeys. May we learn the culture of honoring the kingdom relationships set before our paths. We can see this reflected in Jesus as He went back to visit His hometown in Nazareth. As He returns, He is allowed back into the synagogue, and as He begins to read the scriptures before those who had been familiar with Him since childhood, their reaction to His new revelation is one met with resistance.

I am reminded of the time Jesus went back to His hometown in Nazareth. In Luke 4:14–20 (NIV):

> Jesus returned to Galilee in the power of the Spirit, and news about him spread through the whole countryside. He was teaching in their synagogues, and everyone praised him.
> He went to Nazareth, where he had been brought up, and on the Sabbath day he went into the synagogue, as was his custom. He stood up to read, and the scroll of the prophet Isaiah was handed to him. Unrolling it, he found the place where it is written:

"The Spirit of the Lord is on me,
because he has anointed me
to proclaim good news to the poor.
He has sent me to proclaim freedom for the prisoners
and recovery of sight for the blind,
to set the oppressed free,
to proclaim the year of the Lord's favor.

Then he rolled up the scroll, gave it back to the attendant and sat down. The eyes of everyone in the synagogue were fastened on him. He began by saying to them, "Today this scripture is fulfilled in your hearing."

They all watched and could not understand, as they still only remembered Him as the same Jesus whom they had known since childhood. Perhaps a familiar glimpse came over them as they thought of the boy they had all watched grow up next to them, playing games, going to community feasts and gatherings with them all. As they tried to perceive what these things meant when He spoke as the Son of God, knowing that if they accepted Him as the Messiah, everything was about to change, and perhaps most of them were not ready for such a shift. Perhaps they could not get their imagery off of Jesus, whom they had all seen grow up as a child and into a man. What made Him qualified to call Himself the Son of God? Their anger grew as they considered what this all meant, hostility bred by deception, and thus, they became ready to throw the Promised One off the cliff. How could they have missed this gift that had been brought to them and had been tucked under them for so long? If we keep asking God for pure hearts and a singular lens to see as the Father directs His light to shine over our eyes to see those sent to help us. First, to know Christ's love and communion through His Holy Spirit and then to allow mentors and teachers into our lives that have been sent to help us grow into His likeness.

In similar examples, we can see the relationship that Moses had with Joshua. He allowed Joshua to stand guard outside the tent and gleam from the presence that surrounded them both. Here was Moses' meeting with the Almighty face to face, and Joshua was able to learn by watching the way that Moses would host the presence of God. Joshua honored the gift in Moses and many times followed him even halfway up the mountain when they were on their way to receive the tablets which God had prepared. As described in Exodus 32:17, it appears that Joshua stayed in an abode near the top, waiting for forty days until Moses returned. He was constantly supporting and following the needs of Moses, serving him with all his heart. I believe that his gifting was acquired through serving and learning from his teacher. Over time, Joshua grew in wisdom and favor with the people as well. So much so that by the end of Moses' life, the people became ready to follow Joshua. The fire and zeal that he carried through strong confidence were found in the God that he served under Moses. He knew that God was for him, perhaps because he had built relationship with Him all the while. Joshua knew that the way was already prepared, that he needed only to stand and walk in it. He entered and inherited a land promised to the Israelites, a new territory that his mentor was only allowed to look upon, even after years of roaming together. That's the kind of mentor we all need in our lives, someone who is willing to position themselves under God and then teach us how to hear and follow His instruction on such a high level so we can enter new territory meant for our entire generation.

However, it does not end there. We then must be ready to be mentors to the next generation of sons and daughters that are hungering after more of God. We begin by making ourselves available and approachable, at times even opening the doors for others to feel safe coming to us.

Prayer for God's Fire—Cultivation in Your life

Lord, thank You for the fire that is at Your altar, burning around You as those wheels and spokes are turnings. May our hearts be lit in reverence of You, and may our intimacy with You grow as we keep spending time in Your presence. Help us draw into You like a firefly would be drawn to the light. May we become radiant as we behold You and are drawn more toward You. Lord Jesus, reveal if there is any shame, guilt, and condemnation trying to hide within our hearts. Lead us into a place of safety where we can give You are whole hearts and trust You fully. May Your truth be revealed on every level and every ground of our lives. May the oil in us be increased as we follow You and read Your Word. Lord, we pray for the highest flames to become torches lighting our path and place ambers upon our feet as we stay in reverence of who You are! You are so Holy, and we honor You, King Jesus. Thank You for lighting our hearts on fire for You, Jesus. Thank You for revealing the gifting, which resides in our hearts, and we are ready to serve others to draw all men and women to know You more. Help our race be one of getting to witness and co-release great and wonderful signs and miracles. We love You, and we praise Your great name. Amen.

- CHAPTER 7 -

PEACE BE STILL
THE MOUNTAINS OF VISITATION

The most precious time spent in God's presence will elevate us into a higher awareness that will lead to posturing our hearts into receiving greater measures of His blessings. He wants us to look at where we are standing. Do we view the world through the lens of being surrounded by our circumstances, or do we view it from His elevated place in victory? As we are in Christ, He can share His heart and thoughts with us about strategies to come and movements catching wind upon our lands. He raises us to see things from a higher standard in a place where His grace and mercy are constantly at work.

Ultimately, there is not anywhere found in this universe that God will not travel to meet with His children. We hear of His coming being one of such a humble stance, as He came into a lowly manger on that Christmas day. What a surprise it was for those shepherds to receive such a greeting! Did they look up with marvel and tears in their eyes? How could it be that something so important was going to be entrusted to them first? Who were they? Would anyone even know their name or that they would become touching points for heaven to meet Earth? All that was required of them was found in Him already. They needed only to be present and dare glance upwards. Did they receive the message and follow the instruction given by the heavenly hosts? As they left their flocks, perhaps with others, and journeyed to follow the star that would lead to the Messiah. To eventually find themselves witnessing the most profound miracle, the gift of Jesus. God turned to flesh through His Son and gave up all of Himself so that we could encounter Him on the higher ground again as we learn to ascend to His throne.

The Lord always meets with His children, but He wants to bring us outside of our narrow lens and allow us to view life from the mountaintops. It began with Abraham when he was told by God to lay His only son, Isaac, down as a sacrifice. Ensuring there would be no idols found in his heart. He was commanded to go to Mount Moriah, where he would be tested in his obedience. At this time, Abraham was ready to do as he was told and sacrifice Isaac before the Lord, but God held him back at the very last moment. After seeing that his heart was postured to purely love God in every circumstance, a provision was sent, and a mountain ram was found entangled by its horns. The new sacrifice had been there all along. Why did God choose a ram instead of a lamb? Perhaps because it was symbolic of Christ dying as an adult? When and if looked at closely, rams are adult males that are fully intact. Thus, it was such a symbol of a high place of atonement, which would represent a similar offering made by God Himself as He chose His son, Jesus, and laid Him down on the cross of Calvary to become the final sacrifice for us all. This sacrifice, too, was on a mountain called *Golgotha*, which meant "sculls."

It was on that mountaintop that Abraham was given the vision of the provision that God already made through his final sacrifice of Jesus'

145

life. Yes, he would come as a sacrifice for us to be allowed to enter a higher awareness of the Father's Love. As I pondered the number seven in earlier chapters, it's by no coincidence that God revealed that Chapter 7 would be about His visitations. I believe that seven stood out for our nation as it will continue to become a place of the Lord's Sabbath and rest in His presence to receive higher revelation. Yes, many times, we are not taking the time to rest in the Lord, and therefore, many are getting weary and sick. It's no wonder such a fruitful land has come into some hard times when we have kept running the course with no proper time for rest over our schedules and even our fields. Some farmlands are turned over continuously and not given the time to rest, but God, in His gracious ways, knows how to reconcile our tired, weary bodies and fertilize our lands.

As our lives become completely given to the Lord, we commit all that we have unto Him, including our fields. Remove all idols and places of false worship. We can trust that He alone can release the Shalom over the soil and the land that we walk on regularly. May our foods be re-nourished by the soil that has had time to rest and yield all to its seed. In this chapter, there are specific visitations that God wanted me to speak about that have been instrumental in encountering Him on new levels.

A TESTING—Mt. Langly, CA - A Place of Re-Dedication to God

Our nation has some of the most beautiful Mountain ranges. It's clearly such a painting of brilliant scenery. In our adventures, we have been blessed to live in the Western region and explore the peaks of the Sierra Nevada. Early in our marriage, my husband and I used to live in Tehachapi, California, where we got to enjoy the adventure of very diverse landscapes. In 2009, we found ourselves visiting the beautiful mountains, which included Mt. Langley Peak, next to the highest peak of Mount Whitney. It took many lists in preparation as it was my first time on a backpacking trip, as only minimal items could be carried on our backs up a trail that would lead us to our new mountain retreat. It's amazing how little you need to survive, however, since I had been so accustomed to living in the comfort of modern conveniences for long enough. It felt like we were trying to go back into *The Little House on the Prairie* times, only without the horse carriage to help us chug our belongings up the high hills. It would be three days of hiking as we readied to camp at the Cottonwood lakes, which were about ten miles up into the Sierra Nevada ridge line. Thank God I had been raised in the mountains of Santa Fe with my siblings and cousins, where I had been taught about cliff hikes with only a backpack and food sack to keep us for the day. However, it had been a long time since those childhood adventures. I wondered if I would still have what it took to survive in the wild on bare minimum food, supplies, and clothing.

When the day finally arrived, we loaded our bags and headed up the steep climb as our Honda Civic took us up this humongous ridge leading us into our next adventure. The hiking began as we took our sacks and carried our tents into the trail marked for campers to follow. Our steps began easy and joyful but eventually became a bit harder as our filled backpacks added heavy weight to our weary bodies. We each carried our sleeping gear and all our small essentials, like food, cooking pots, matches, clothing, and fishing gear. We had a bear canister, where we planned to store all our dry food, and our water purifier, where we could collect clean water and have it cleansed for drinking. Have you ever watched a survivor episode? Imagine an episode with two newlyweds who were still getting to know each other. It was kind of like that, just no actual cameras around us, but us two and our giant sacks on our backs, and miles of trails up a mountain that we were exploring for the first time. I can't believe I said yes to this trip. Perhaps my curiosity got the best of me on this one, but it surely was a time that I will never forget, as I still have memories of the beautiful sights and the pristine air at the top of some of these spectacular peaks. The pure glacier water that melted from the snow tops freezing cold but so clear that you could see the swimming schools of golden trout. Have you ever noticed that God's most beautiful destinations seem to be places that barely get visited because sometimes it's placed on high peaks that are hard to get to? I think God likes to show off and does it quite often just to show me how creative and marvelous He is. He sets His paintbrush to work and, at times, wants me to know that it's set up perfectly in such a way that He chooses to share that one spectacular portrait with us as we set ourselves to go higher.

Spiritually, this is very much the case when I have chosen to give Him my all and pursue Him first above everything else. Then, He releases His sweet grace over my heart's pursuit as He so longs for time with us all. He lets us dive in and then unilaterally releases His presence over those areas of our lives where we seek His favor in our lives. That mountain can be a revelation of His deep love. It's always been there; I may have even looked at it from a far distance and acknowledged its existence. But on this day, I finally decided to get up close and personal, to put my feet upon the paths that would take me higher, which opened the door to infinite wonder and exuberant radiance. With my husband's encouragement, I peered over that treasured mountain and saw its splendor from within, so vibrant, filled with life, and every contour of light it beheld as the light rays shown upon its ridge lines were connectors to my Father in heaven. He created it all so that I would, on these three days, explore the marvelous sights and sounds as only a child could do. I was in love with a man whom God had chosen and trusted that our journey together would be blessed by God as we ventured into His created wild expanse.

For two days, we fished, laughed, made fires, swam in cold lakes, cuddled under the tent, and began to enjoy what life felt like to be on our very own, away from everything that had previously taken our time. No expectations up above the tree line, where the oxygen got very slim. It was a place where time seemed to also disappear, and a day felt like ten days. We could really speak to God and feel as if He spoke back through every chirping bird and every leaf that rustled in the wind. It became a great escape. I marveled at His glorious creation even more.

We could have probably stayed on this mountain our whole lives if it wasn't for the third day when we had an encounter that caused us to both rethink our mountain strategy. We were getting closer to evening time. We had finished grilling our fish for dinner and cleaning our pan near our tent. We had followed our normal routine, except this time, we didn't clean our camp well enough. We left fish oil around the rock next to the tent. We had hidden our bear canister one hundred feet away from us and then began settling into our humble tent for the night. We prepared ourselves for another comfy night of rest. However, this night was not at all like any of the previous ones. We said our bedtime prayers and had our night story caps, then were fast asleep. At about 1:30 a.m., I was awakened by what sounded like a giant tongue licking a puddle of water on a nearby rock. It sounded like a twelve-foot monster as its slurping kept drawing all the fish oil into his trap, then the ground began shaking, and the rustling of leaves got closer. It sounded like steps were approaching steadily. Immediately, every sense in my body was heightened as sudden adrenaline was being pumped into my heart. The smell of wet urine, like that of a feral animal, got so close that I could smell and sense he was right next to my tent. It so happened that I glanced right into my newlywed husband's eyes as he glared over with a look of complete horror. He did not have to say a word, for he was already relaying a very strong message, "Don't *move!*" I froze in silence as the grizzly sharp paws began to search for something in my backpack, which lay outside our very dainty home. At this point, I felt like a wink of my life began to flash before my eyes. I knew that the only thing between me and this wild bear was a small wall of plastic

PEACE BE STILL THE MOUNTAINS OF VISITATION

covers, a fraud of safety, which held no true substantial strength in its weak woven fabric borders. This was not how I had envisioned the end of the story to be written out.

And so, in an instant, began the night of my pleading with God. I gazed into the heavens through a small triangular opening on the top of that flimsy shelter. In the most convincing attempt, I asked my Creator to cover our lives. I knew that I had not lived it to the fullest measure of His honor and glory. I knew that I had not given Him everything and I would be ending this life early. It was certain that I needed to have more areas seared by His fire, so I could do more to help advance His kingdom plans upon this Earth. Something inside me knew that I was still withholding many truths from Him. My house was not completely His, there were rooms that I had locked in my heart, and at this moment, I knew that I had to live to make things right with my Lord. I asked my King, first, for forgiveness. I asked if He would give me a second chance, and I would be sure to give Him my all on every level and ground. I believe He heard my cries that night as a tear ran down my face. For some reason, I knew I wasn't ready to meet my Father yet, I had recognized that my life was near a crossroads, and it was now or never to choose Him to the fullest measure.

That night, a hungry bear made up its mind, perhaps after receiving instructions from His Creator that we were not its diner, as he waded around us a couple of times and then walked away to go fishing instead. We finally came out of our tent, holding up our flashlights and waving our arms up high, but it was nowhere in sight. We had been spared and given another chance. We had to now make every moment count, for our Father had shone His mercy and grace! We had to wait until morning for us to be able to descend the mountain and head back to the car. It was hard waiting until that morning arrived, we did not sleep that night, and I never wanted to go camping after that again unless I had a cabin or truck to sleep in. However, over time the Lord, in His goodness, healed the trauma of that bear encounter.

What are the final moments of our lives going to feel like? Perhaps we can take account early and not find ourselves at such a crossroads as I was on this cold night? We need to take a solid step into our Father's heavenly kingdom. We cannot straddle the lines of complacency and hold on to the worldly ways which feel comfortable. As a nation, we are at a crossroads. We must make our decision to be all in for Christ. There is not going to be an entrance into heaven by any other means but through Christ Jesus alone. He is the only way into the Father's House. In John 14:6 (ESV), Jesus said to him, "I am the way, and the truth, and the life. No one comes to the father except through me." The Lord is taking us to a mountain of decisions. Where we can see Him in clarity and absorb His radical grace as we submit all our hearts and ways to Him. He is able to exceed unto greater measures, and His goodness is better than we could comprehend unless it is revealed to us. Read Ephesians 3:14–19 (NKJV). His Word takes us into a higher dimension where His goodness is an ensemble of His sun rays coming upon our lives and every morning renewing us daily. What a graceful Daddy we have.

Assembling of the Saints-Communion in Christ Unity
New Ringgold, PA

The mountain passages through Pennsylvania had become some of our favorite places to visit. However, when I heard about the place in Ringgold, PA, I stopped and pondered. I had never seen or heard of such a place on the map. An invitation from a friend opened the door of opportunity. She was going to retreat into the Mountains at a place called Blue Mountain Christian Retreat with a group of people that were going to seek God on higher ground. She was leading much of the administration of the trip details, thus having one special reservation that allowed a friend to come along with her. At the time, all I could do was desire after more I had tasted, and now I wanted to enter God's presence deeper and learn more about Him. I knew that I needed to retreat away to be with the Lord and gain deeper insight into his heart away from distractions. For a mother, home educator, and student to truly retreat with God, it must be ordained and planned. However, God usually sets us up for unexpected surprises. Expediently, we said yes, to the call, and I drove up those spectacular woodsy roads in great wonder.

The retreat for me began early, as it took me a couple of hours to get up the Pennsylvania Mountain ridge. It was spectacular, as colors glistened in the sun, a beautiful canvas for my whole senses. I drove and talked to God the whole way. At times, I worshipped, and then, I just conversed with the Creator of the universe. He was kind, gentle, funny, and sorted things out as we talked. It's the kind of thing He does on our road trips. He speaks to me through His creation, at times through signs, and at other times completely by giving me His perspective on certain matters that I've been asking about. By the time I got there and zoomed up the driveway, I was ready to start a mountaintop connection with Him. I knew he had brought me here to teach me so much more, and boy was I right. The views from the conference hall were regal. It felt like the best of both worlds, fanciful and mountaineering, fitting into a perfect image for my heart's delight.

I readily met up with a group of acquaintances that had started to connect, it was four friends who had come together in a small cabin, and they had made room for me in their adventure. We gathered and spent some time reconnecting, sharing stories and testimonies, and drawing out our faith. Then we prepared for a gathering on top of the mountain in a quaint chapel, where we were excited to hear a few ministers that were humble vessels pouring out oil of exuberant kingdom news, and thus our adventures began. What joy I felt when I got there and saw familiar faces of people I knew. This had to be a divine setup.

Like hungry inquisitive children, we listened to the word as it calibrated soul and mind into Christ's victory. It was a moment drawn to perfection. He had been fitting, tucking, clipping, molding, and shaping my heart and my mind into His love, like an eagle being fashioned and conditioned for a race. This meeting on this mountain was a call higher to ignite our flame into forward motion and a description of how we all fit together into His perfect plan.

In the evening, Dr. Jenkins introduced our first speaker, an extraordinary man who emphasized the importance of forgiveness and deep love in Christ. Eman Norman spoke as the sky was lit with immeasurable stars glistening in the night sky. The example he shared was sobering as he endured trials and overcame depression after his wife had left him for his brother. However, through Christ's unwavering love, he was able to find forgiveness in his heart for all, including himself. So much more of his testimony can be read in his book titled *Kingdom of Loving.* The Lord had walked him through endurance and love that became an obvious anointing flowing like sweet honey and setting captives free from unforgiveness. This young man had found his ultimate purpose and was sharing Christ's love and healing power with so many people. Like Paul in prison, he triumphed over his prison and taught others how to break free into relationships.

Dr. Jenkins has a friend that we all called Momma Moses for a good reason. As she walked around the room with staff and hit the ground as we prayed together in the spirit, she churned the atmosphere and broke off the timidity, and dissolved the sand off our sandals. Every disappointment melted off like chaff. We became motivated by a charge in the air. Holy Spirit became a whirlwind and took our prayers higher into the throne room, then enveloped us like mist. She ministered with such authority; it was incredible to be among the hundred chosen by God for this experience. Dr. Jenkins called us all into our positions as soldiers in this end-time harvest. We knew we were putting our feet to the fire as we all stepped forward and expressed our yes before the Almighty! Our faith was resurrected, and we felt like eagles soaring upwind, hearing the words of our Father as He gave us insight into things to come and things to follow.

At the end of the night service, we gathered with a group of believers and followed the Lord's leading to take communion together in a friend's bunker house. Seven of us all came into that home, but there was one among us who was mighty and powerful that led us to break bread in an intimate setting. He had us first confess our sins to one another, and without hesitation, we released the weights that easily held us up. Hebrews 12:1 (NKJV):

> Therefore we also, since we are surrounded by so great a cloud of witnesses, let us lay aside every weight, and the sin which so easily ensnares *us,* and let us run with endurance the race that is set before us.

As we shared these areas of weakness, our brotherly unity formed in prayer and encouragement as we saw the blanket of the Holy Spirit cover our frailties and clothe us with amazing love. After prayer, we took the bread and the wine together, and the home became filled with a glory-like fog that wrapped the whole cabin. We fell off our chairs as we were being filled with joy! We truly felt the love for each other intensify as if we knew that God was our witness to this new bond He had formed in us seven. What was the Lord calling us together to build or do?

The next day we awakened and went to a mid-morning service. The minute I arrived, I came to the door, and as I was passing by Eman, who had ministered the previous night, I felt the Love of God radiate from upon his life and enter mine. I began to weep as I just felt God's love heightened. My heart was receiving more love than it had before.

The love that God wanted me to know He had poured over this minister was breathtaking. It was that day that I opened my ears wide to hear all that He had to say. When He ministered about forgiveness and loving His enemies, I knew it was an actual life He had learned to live before He came to share about it. He had been given much authority in forgiveness and love, so much so that God wanted to make me aware of the love he walked in and imparted. It broke through every hardened slate of my own heart; tears were the only thing I could release in response to this enormous love of God. Therefore, our messages cannot just be written based on the perception of watching others go through something. They have got to become living examples of lessons we have learned because we have first walked through the fire ourselves. This is going to have to become the way that we minister in this hour. We need to come with real authority and speak in all power so that the captives are released and set free from their own chains.

After service, we all took time together at lunch, and Evangelist Eman came and sat with me at a table just to check on how I was doing. I kept weeping as I told him I didn't know I needed all this love. He smiled and just reassured me that God was good and things around me were going to be changing. What I believe occurred after our communion night of taking on the body and the blood with other believers softened my heart from all hardened, callous spots and massaged my senses to receive the fullest measure of love that needed to pierce through to bring about a renewal in my heart and mind.

I had to first forgive myself and others who had brought harm to me, especially previous church hurts. God was then able to wash me with this love in such a way that catapulted me into freedom to soar to the highest peaks of this beautiful mountain. The lessons on this mountain were some of tremendous perspective. To remain free in flight, we must periodically take a moment to open our hearts through communion in Christ to view and ask the hard questions. Am I holding anything against my brothers or sisters? Is there any unforgiveness in me that could hold me back? When really searched, this could be the very key that opens us up to receive the greater measures of His healing touch. Ephesians 3:14–19 (NKJV):

> For this reason I bow my knees to the Father of our Lord Jesus Christ, from whom the whole family in heaven and earth is named, that He would grant you, according to the riches of His glory, to be strengthened with might through His Spirit in the inner man, that Christ may dwell in your hearts through faith; that you, being rooted and grounded in love, may be able to comprehend with all the saints what is the width and length and depth and height—to know the love of Christ which passes knowledge; that you may be filled with all the fullness of God.

Prayer: Father, search our hearts and open us up to You, and if there is any area of unforgiveness found in our hearts, Lord, help us to forgive those who have trespassed against us. Help us to forgive ourselves and then also forgive those who have sinned again us and brought harm to our lives. We chose to release and forgive with Your help, Father, and as we give You these areas that need Your forgiveness, we ask You to apply your precious blood upon these sins and wash us clean. Thank You for the union of being completely one with You, Jesus. Thank You for releasing us from these setbacks. Father, we receive Your perfect love. May it cover us with so much warmth, and may it shine brilliantly over our whole lives. Amen.

Ghana—A Journey of Faith and Obedience

It was a huge step of faith to say yes when God called me to go to Ghana! Some may say, well, it's not such a hard place to get to, and there are many Christians already there. This is true. However, the fact that I had never been on the mission field before was a miracle. Also, the timing of the whole thing accounts for a miracle. During the peak of a pandemic that struck our nation like a thief in the night, I was stuck in my own basement, recovering from COVID. The days had grown so long as I was quarantined for a full ten days away from my family. About halfway through this time, all I could do was lay in a weakened state, trying to gain my strength back.

One night, I began to really feel my heart straining just to get air into my lungs; my chest was feeling pressed in, and I began to feel like I was drowning from the inside out. It was the worst feeling I've ever experienced, and the pain that was coming from my nerves into my body, especially the back of my right knee, which had become inflamed and swollen at the point of hinging as the pain had migrated to that joint. It was at that point that I was praying and asking God for help when I was visited by the Lord's angel, whom I sensed entered the room and came to my bedside. Then I saw through a spiritual lens. The angel was there for my protection, as well as for encouragement. I was feeling so lonely and wondering if this is how many people were dying across the US, with no family to love them or care for them. It was hard as suffering was sucking my bones dry, and loneliness depleted my hope reserves. Normally I've always been a glass-half-full kind of gal, but in this scenario, I was very empty. It could have felt very easy to just give up. However, the Lord knew that I just needed a word of encouragement, He wanted me to know that He was watching over my breath and it would not be snatched away a minute early before I completed all that He asked of me. I received a phone call the next day from our pastor, who confirmed that as she prayed for me, she acknowledged that an angel was sent. Well, this angel came with a new assignment and began to instruct me to plan my trip to the nation of Africa.

It was a few years prior the Lord God had orchestrated placing a mentor that I highly valued in my life. I just couldn't understand the connections yet. In following the lead of the Holy Spirit, I wrote and asked if this was the right time to visit his nation. I was pleasantly surprised by the response; his team had been seeking God in prayer and had heard from heaven that two people were being sent to their nation. I believe only the Lord could have opened such a window at such an uncertain time. In that same month, I received a five-year visa approval for travel. I received a clean health record, I received full funding from kingdom investors for the flight and added blessings to bring along as a mission offering. I also made connection with a ministry that was very connected with my friends out in Ghana. This was confirmation of the Lord's plans as he had me meet people from Ghana in every area. Before I was scheduled to leave, my doctor's office ran tests to make sure I was clear of all viruses. At this medical facility, the doctor that was seeing me was a doctor from Ghana, who gave me great insight into the nation. I also visited a bank where I needed to plan for the correct currency, and again, there, I met a person from Ghana at the currency exchange. It was all very strategic by the Lord's doing. It was his way of giving me assurance that I was on the right path. By the beginning of December, I was traveling to Ghana in a plane that had been prepared in advance, and the strength that was being built in my trust in God had skyrocketed. I felt like I could do anything with God as my director and protector.

Yes, you did hear me correctly. I was flying on my own. I would not recommend this to anyone, especially when you're going into a mission field. You should always take a team to go with you. The beautiful friend, whom I had invited, did not make it immediately due to unforeseen purposes. She did, however, arrive a week after. This did not catch God off guard. I believe it was a setup. In my case, this was a test of my faith and trust. Did God really say? In this situation, many called and gave me their advice. You should not go alone. It's not safe. The voice in my heart kept increasing. I could hear God say, "You're traveling with my authoritative rights, as I am the one who called you on this trip. Thus, I am your protection." This was the comfort I traveled with.

At one point, I will say it was an interesting interception as intimidation tried to get in. When I was mid-way to Ghana, in the

Amsterdam airport, a clerk at the desk looked at my flight ticket and then asked me who are you traveling with to Ghana? He looked around me and said, it is not safe for you to travel on your own. Quickly, I responded and said what makes you think I am traveling alone? I am in great company by the almighty. Holy Spirit is right next to me. He is leading the way, and he goes ahead anywhere that he sends me to go. He then said, "Oh, I do not see Him. In that case, alright! You and your imaginary friend can pass on." I felt a bit of a zing come into me as I pushed off the hindrance and walked away, sitting down in a seat next to other families that looked like they were on the right plane to get home to Ghana. Many looked twice when they saw me, but it was simply in curiosity. I was ready for a joyful experience. What did God have in mind for me to learn through all this?

I was pleasantly surprised by the honor and respect that I received upon my arrival and throughout my whole two weeks spent there. Pastor David Agyepong of International Life Giving Church arrived at the airport with Apostle Richmond. Both walked with such confidence and grace when they came to me and said hello. I could feel the warmth and protection of the Lord surrounding them. They are both men of great stature, filled with Christ's authority and love. They led me to their vehicle and took my bags into their car, and we began our journey together. The entire trip was so impactful. I felt that God wanted me to understand and learn my value in Him first. If He chose me as a vessel, who was I to call the King wrong, even if I may have felt the least qualified? Many times, as I sat on the front row or arrived ready to minister at a certain church, I was covered in so much prayer that it alone carried me to Christ's victory and His finished work on the cross. At times, it took us an hour to arrive at specific locations that required us to minister. In the time of driving, we were also praying in very high-level spiritual tongues. The spirit was removing any lack and weakness in me during this time so that when we arrived, we were now completely hidden in Christ, ready to just be the vessels to pour through. A deep consecration was taking place in me, deeper than I can explain. I was being carried forward and higher by their deep intercessions and powerful anointed prayers.

I was also being treated like royalty, like someone of great significant value. It was so humbling to have amazing men and women of God pour over my life in such a way that I often whispered to God, "I do not deserve this level of service or sacrifice." It initially made me want to reject the offerings of meals cooked, rides given, clothing made in my perfect size, and so much more. It was then that God reminded me that He could have chosen anyone He wanted for this job. He said it could have been your daughter, who is nine years old. All it required was a big yes. So, in just the first few days that I was there, my heart was overwhelmed by the love that God showered through His amazing servants and ministers. They were doing this for the King of Glory, and it was obvious that they knew Him well.

We began walking through the neighborhoods in advance. I followed Pastor David around and saw his heart for the community as he provided for the families and the children everywhere he went. He visited the widows and the homes of anyone sick among them, and with any amount he had, he gave of himself. He poured his heart into the young men and women in ministry every day, directly understanding the needs around them in the mission field. The demonstration of their love for the community made such a huge impact on me. This pastor loved his church with an agape love with no desire to gain anything back and gave up his life for those in the church and community to give others a chance to know Christ. It was the first step to being entrusted to speak to this community. I had to have Christ's love for them first. The posture of my heart was tremendously softened, and I cried an entire day straight as the love of God flowed in waves of His blessings into the fabric of my calling. Many times, missionaries can get deceived when they think that they are the gift from God being sent, and they think that they are going to bring so much change but haven't even taken time to ask God for the actual word over each specific region and church first.

The journey continued with me asking God for the letters (messages He had) to those churches. He then would take me into a deep love encounter and speak to me about the things that they were doing that really pleased Him. He would release me to commend them in areas that were working well. Then after showing me their strengths, He would then change course and show me areas that were still needing improvement. Lastly was the promised reward. Through His help and leading, it was a similar process used by Apostle John in Revelation as he wrote letters to the seven churches, addressing the strengths and weaknesses. Most of these encounters or downloads would come in the early morning hours before the day could even begin.

In the first church, I was most worried because it was the church where the bishop and eldest brother resided. I thought if I got this wrong, they might not allow me to go into any of the other churches. So, when the Lord brought me to a childhood memory, I began to share about a time when I lived in the mountains of Santa Fe, and I was tending to the chickens in the coop. I remembered a very territorial rooster who did not let me leave the coop after I had already picked up the eggs. He guarded that hen house with his life, and in my zeal as a little girl, I decided to have a showdown with that stubborn rooster. I stared him down and held my basket tightly. I then charged toward him to intimidate him into backward movement. He began to flap his wings and ran straight for me. It was hilarious from the outside view but scary from a child's eyes. He came straight for my eyes and pecked my forehead as I ran out of the coop, then I came out with all eggs in tow. My sister looked at me and said, "What happened to your forehead?" she pointed, and I wiped my head to find that there was a huge burst of blood coming from my head. The rooster had pecked me so hard that it had created a bump that I would have for weeks. But the point of that story was made, that even when the enemy tries to distract or derail our assignment, we should always move forward at all costs, knowing that God is our protection and will lead us right through any battle. Even if I had a battle wound, I felt the protection of my father, and it earned me a badge of courage, knowing that I could do all things through Christ, who gives me strength (Philippians 4:13).

This church I was visiting was a church that had its eyes on the prize and was moving forward despite all setbacks. They had overcome much, and I could feel God's pleasure over them. God shared with them that He was getting ready to send the rains in ways that they had only been dreaming of. Their resilience to keep pushing was a mark of achievement they had obtained. This church was ushering in a great move, and in their obedience to God, they had captured His blessings. However, God wanted them to step into new ground with the gifts of spiritual infilling. Thus the movement of the Spirit needed to have more freedom to move. The Lord would release them of all fear of being undignified before man and instead get low and get filled with more of His presence. I sensed that this church already walked under the understanding of the power of God, but God was getting ready to break new ground with this church, a greater manifestation of His miracles and wonders was ready to be poured out. It really marked me, and I still think of them and pray for them often. A few days later, it also rained in torrential ways that I don't think I had ever witnessed before, in the same manner as the rain coming down on the new soil of Africa. To me, it was a sign of blessing that God was doing something amazing in the city of Koforidua, Ghana.

Atwea Mountain—Partnering with Angels

Some of the most important lessons I learned were on this mountain we visited called Atwea, a prayer Mountain of God's presence, where I saw the effects of fervent powerful prayers impacting the nations of the world. This journey we were on took us a whole day of driving and hiking to make it to the top of an existing prayer area, where many pilgrims come from around the world to seek God on higher ground. The mission built on the mountain is a Methodist church, as the mountain was used between 1959–1965 to journey among travelers overlooking the Atwea village. Then eventually became a prayer mountain after Rev. Abraham Osei Asibey had a revelation as a cloud draped over the top of the mountain while he visited Atwea. He was called by the Lord to pilgrimage to the top, where he experienced an extraordinary encounter with God's presence. He describes it as a mount of transfiguration as he heard the voice of God and he received a glimpse of the glory of God. Today there is a cross that has been a marker where the presence was experienced (Ampaw-Asiedu Aug 2010).

Walking to the top was beautiful and felt invigorating. My friend Maureen, who arrived a week later, caught up to us and was able to journey with us to the top. The Lord was able to take her to an extraordinary level of restoration as the journey up was hard, but the journey back down brought healing from fear of heights. Pastor David brought a great team that led us up the mountain and prepared for us to stay for the night right on top, where the holy altar was set for prayer. Our guides knew the trails well and had been there before, which brought us much comfort as it was great knowing we were not alone.

In the beginning, we reached the top and saw the mission church that was set up as a place of worship. However, most of the time, it was closed for special ceremonies or church use. Most people came and prayed together in the bush, where there were separate solitary places in the offshoots found to be places where true unity in prayer could be obtained. We gathered and prayed together for hours, taking the Word of God with us, and began to read scripture while then meditating over each scripture as the Lord brought light into our hearts. When it began to get later in the day, we went back to the central prayer area and rented some mats where we would lay for the night when we got weary. We began to intercede and spend time with the Lord. As I prayed over the mountain top, I had a beautiful vision of a mighty fiery angel who partnered with our prayers as we spoke in our heavenly language, and in quickness, like a lightning bolt, this angel went forward to guide the pathway for the prayer to be successful. I felt the Lord's presence as these mighty anointed angels were coming in from every side of the mountain and partnering with prayers of all the saints. It went on for a good while, and I felt my voice getting louder and louder until I was almost shouting and eventually wore myself out. Enough that I came back for a while to our camp to take a rest.

At about one o'clock in the morning, I was awakened when I heard loud prayers rising from many pilgrims who were lifting their highest offering to the Lord. I rose and looked across the top of the dark mountain, now filled with a mist, as dim lights shone through the crowds. I noticed some deliverances were taking place, and some were weeping as they lay before the Lord. It became such a deep memory in my reference as I saw in a vision a whirlwind coming down, and the prayers were immerging into a tunnel that was carrying the prayers of the saints from the past and present into the heavenlies.

A holy fear was upon me as I just uttered in spiritual tongues and felt my prayers joining the orchestra of those who were warring and had come before me. I knew this was a place of great convergence, and I was encountering God's Holy throne. All things I said up there were taken by His heavenly hosts straight into the realms of His glory. Oh, how near it felt to be next to him on this mountain, I did not want to go back to sleep, and somehow, I happened to still slip back into a rest as I pulled my one sheet cover over my whole body and took a few deep breaths and found myself back at rest. It truly was a mount of transfiguration, a place of deep encounter with God's glory.

There remains much work left to be done in Koforidua, Ghana. My heart is that pastor David will receive all the funding needed to purchase lands in the mountains and build the dream center the Lord has called him to lead, a church that will be an epicenter and will include an education department, a health center, and all their medical needs met. A place where orphans and widows are cared for and will receive all the resources that they require to live a healthy abundant life. Where their souls can be strengthened in faith and their bodies nourished to fulfill the great commission over all of Africa. May this dream become a reality as the Lord releases the greatest blessing over His faithful servants in this hour. The investments to come shall be led by the Lord in every aspect and shall have great returns upon the soil of God's servants. The connections God is making with Africa and the US are purposeful. As we continue to see His ministers come bearing good news, they are standing in the gaps for our nation in prayer as they contend for the Lord's restoration.

- CHAPTER 8 -

A MOVEMENT THROUGH INTERCESSORS

As our nation begins to bend knee before the Lord in full submission, He begins to open our eyes to areas that need His presence. We can then begin to enter covenant prayer with others who are seeking the Lord earnestly for restoration and healing over their city, state, and nation. Over the last couple of years, we partook in a current movement led by intercessors of a united forum in Florida. And began to see that there are networks across the globe that are pressing into seeking after the Father's heart in unity with others who are in synchronization with a new movement being born. The Lord spoke to our hearts that if more states followed this similar blueprint, our nation would see much more healing and unity. How pleasing it is when we all come together into unity for the benefit of seeing Christ's revelation over an entire city and nation. Psalm 133:1 (NIV):

> How good and pleasant it is when brothers live together in unity! It is like precious oil poured on the head, running down on the beard, running down on Aaron's beard, down upon the collar of his robes. It is as if the dew of Hermon were falling on Mount Zion.

The Unity of One Voice—Florida

We were visiting Florida on assignment from the Lord. We had just spent a few days at the Light the Fire Again Conference in Orlando, where they had just announced that they were opening a new church called Nations Church. The connections we made also led us to attend a few different churches as we were there. We visited a church in Kissimmee, FL, where the pastor had been connected to our home church apostle for years prior to his moving out to this state. Our team released our decrees over the congregation and began to pray strongly over the state for both rain and the Lord's revival fire. We felt the Lord's pleasure over the state and noticed that the congregants were hungry and ready in position, however a bit low in attendance. This, of course, was due to the pandemic they had just gone through, having some members come back after sickness. A symbol happening across the nation, many churches experienced a leveling down of onsite attendance and a higher proportion of attendees online.

After sharing with the pastor our traveling plans across the US in intercessions leading us to pray for revival and reformation, he immediately made the connections and shared a few of his intercessors' phone numbers with us. We called one of his intercessors and immediately prayed with one on the phone. The second one was a beautiful lady who also spoke to my husband and received all our information. She felt the need to ask us if we could connect with her and her husband before we left the state. We eagerly found ourselves in a small rural town in the center of Florida called Intercession City. It seemed surreal that we would be meeting some strong prayer warriors in a place that had such a significant history when it came to revival over the state.

When we met with these amazing generals in the faith, we met outside an old Wesleyan Methodist church that we knew had tremendous history. We could feel the prayers that had been released over the grounds. Even before we talked to them, we were very excited and felt God's orchestration of such a meeting. They came to us as if they had known us our whole lives, and a connection in the spirit was formed quickly as, by the Lord's leading, they became instant apostolic parents. We were added to their prayer list as we continued our journey across the states. Again, only something that God could do. We knew this was only the beginning of a lifelong relationship with amazing leaders as well as teachers.

Over time, we were able to attend one of their conferences in Florida, which involved learning more about the pursuit of the Father's vision over their prayer network. The heart that these powerful intercessors carry is to bring unity in Christ's love and transform the state through His power and presence. Their idea was to bring kingdom alignment and vision across the state by connecting intercessors with different leaders who represented the seven mountains of influence.

Intercession City: The Ark of the Covenant

In the 1920s, this city we visited used to be called Interocean City, and it was originally developed in hopes of making it a tourist attraction that would have canals running from the Atlantic to the Gulf Coast. Originally there were plans to build a large hotel that would become an addition to an amusement park, as it would be a major tourist attraction. However, the great depression hit our nation, and the building project ceased. Only the hotel was now sitting empty for ten years until Bishop Osie England from Virginia came and purchased the property and began her great work of turning it into a Christian University for Missionaries. Many came to attend, and eventually, the town drew many Intercessors that came to call the Wesleyan church their home. Those who sought after praying for the needs of others and seeking God together for the harvest to be made plentiful. Eventually, the town became known as Intercession City, as it was a hub for intercessors to be sent from America to the nations.

Today this town has gone through much hardship, and its population has dwindled down to an estimated 600. It remains in need of revitalization and restoration. The intercessors we met have received great vision to bring a renewal into the heart of Florida as they draw up their plans to bring the Lord's ark into the center of their town. What does this all mean? Exactly what it sounds like. They are building blueprints to have a full-sized replica of the Lord's ark, which will be found in the center of the town. It will serve as a place where people can come and rest and take time in the Lord's presence. We are lifting this couple up in our prayers and ask you to also join in prayer and believe with us in faith. You can read more about Intercession City and find historical accounts of the changes that this city has brought to our nation.[14]

It is such a symbol of what God is doing in our nation and in the heart of our United States. Though it may appear to have been stripped of all its glory due to the reports of division and disunity, there are different reports from separate perspectives. Those who are part of the world with an agenda to spew fear into the heart of man, and then there is the other, those with the heart of the Father. These are the remnants that are of a higher lineage, one of Christ's suffering and resurrection power. These are marching forward to bring the light into all darkness to distinguish it and restore the Lord's plans for our nation. We must open our hearts and prepare the altar to house the holy presence of the Lord's Shekinah glory again. Every state must assemble its prayer lines and begin to pray in such a union that will release great results. It's our job to learn how to pray effective, fervent prayers that will avail much (James 5:16).

Prophetic Insight—The Rod of Authority
Moravian Falls, NC

On April 2021, a group from our church traveled to a conference at Moravian Falls, NC. We spent some amazing time with a congregation seeking the Lord under a prophetic atmosphere. As we attended a church called The Gathering, under Morningstar ministries, we received so much insight and revelation into the heart of the Father in reference to our access to his authority by faith. As the first speaker, who was leading the conference, began to minister, I received a word from the Lord as she spoke. He softly challenged me and asked if I could see the two angels at her side. When I leaned into His Word, I asked the Lord to open my eyes, that I may see them. I became awe-struck as I saw the giant angels on each side of her, they were taller than the building, and I could only see them from the waist down as their upper bodies peered above the ceiling. I leaned over to a friend sitting next to me and explained to her what I was witnessing. She just smiled and nodded her head as kindly as possible. I marveled at God's creation.

A few moments after my vision, the minister began to share with us her first encounter in an open field in the Moravian Mountains. As she was hiking, she came to a place of seeing two angels that were assigned to her and were clothed like Native Americans, imagery of the history of this place came to my heart. The group consisted of African descendants, Colonists, and Cherokees, who were part of the original formation of the brotherly faith assemblies, developing strong values and stable trade. These angels were guardians of the mountain and were partnered in making sure the will of the father was accomplished throughout this minister's life.

A hundred years before Martin Luther began the protestant reformation, there was a faith group of Bohemians from the Moravians in the Czech Republic who traced their roots to 1450 after the martyrdom of Jan Hus. In 1522 the brethren traveled to seek asylum in Germany and were housed by Count Nicholas Louis Von Zinzendorf, a religious leader. Due to religious wars, Moravians were almost wiped out during the 1600s. However, under Zinzendorf, a group remained that became the first protestant missionaries, expanding their base into Europe and the British colonies. In 1730 they traveled with the colonies into Northern Pennsylvania and acquired land in two settlements called Nazareth and Bethlehem. The Moravians also purchased about 100,000 acres owned by Lord Granville near the banks of Muddy Creek in Piedmont, North Carolina.[15] In the heart of Wilkes County, a band of brothers found a beautiful Mountain, which glistened as a waterfall spouted forth and named it Moravian Falls in 1753. Later, in 1760 they purchased a town called Salem, meaning peace, and established a strong community in the backwoods of NC.

After the meeting, I took a break to walk outside the building, as I had heard friends speak about a burial ground hidden on site for the late prophet Bob Jones. I asked the Holy Spirit if I could go to the grounds, and He said to walk around the building and follow my lead. So, I prayed and walked around the building, He highlighted a direction, and a specific landmark stood out to me. I glanced over the field of wild grass and overgrown woods and began making my way to the location highlighted. As I got to the first area, I was praying in the spirit when He said to keep going to the next tree. By this time, I could barely see the church building. It was invigorating as I ventured to explore with the Spirit leading my every step. I finally arrived and noticed that the gravestones were tucked into a perfect grove. I sat under a tree on a bench and just breathed in the air and gazed in peaceful absolute assurance. Of course, I would find it if He was leading the way. There is no missing a thing. The clarity in hearing Him this precise was refreshing.

Something that caught my attention was an iron rod that came from his graveside. It was later similarly found along the prayer mountain, as stories were shared that at every meeting site with God, Prophet Jones would lay a rod into the ground and label it with a red marker. An established marker of a God-magnitude visitation. It reminded me of Joshua 4:19, when Joshua led the Israelites across the Jordan, then set markers by laying twelve stones of remembrance after having grand God encounters. I also kept hearing the song in my heart, rooted, and grounded in love, hey. The root of a healthy tree should grow down in its strength before it then expands its branches so that it can support all the growth and fruit it's set to bare.

For an entire year after this journey, I would continue to learn about God's rod of authority. In Psalm 23, we hear of the shepherd's rod as it is used to correct and guide the sheep. He is guiding us every step and forming our character alike to His image daily. But we have got to be pliable and stay teachable. I believe that God was shaping my faith to believe that His Word was a firm rod deeply rooting my heart to His. His words were written and sealed in my heart and were established by the authority of His right arm. Psalm 138:2 (NKJV): "I will worship toward Your holy temple and praise Your name For Your lovingkindness and Your truth; For You have magnified Your word above all Your name."

Restoring Our Allegiance to God

It is through Christ that He enables us to rebuild the foundations of our nation by laying the stones of faith and restoring the gates of the Lord's temple in our lives. The dedication of the temple and the reading of the book that had for so long been missing. The book of Nehemiah in 2 Kings is the perfect illustration of His guidelines for restoration. Having a plan and a vision requires us to write down what we are hearing and then calculate everything it will take to build back the ruins. We must come into agreement with God's Word, as its prophetic insight throughout its pages has carried the plan for full redemption and healing. That includes our personal, communities, and national spheres. If we unify our heartbeat to Christ's plans, we will take our land back and begin the process of rebuilding. We will be unashamed to read the Word of God at the assembly until every person has heard and begins to shine with the truth.

Understanding will come upon our nation as the seven spirits of revelation clothe our leaders (Revelation 5:6). We will also learn to speak words of life and power, not destruction or doom. Instead of calling down fire on each other gripped by anger or revenge, we'll be careful not to gain a name for ourselves, as sons of thunder did in rage (Mark 3:17). Instead, by gaining wisdom, we can learn from the prophet Elijah in 1 Kings 18:38, as he was calling fire down after he had restored the altar of God. That fire became a righteous fire set to bring awareness of the power of God as the highest authority. All idols were exposed and expelled after the evidence of God interrupted their assembly. Every person fell face down and began to repent and worship the one true God.

We stand at a crossroads again, as we have seen so many idols elevated and worshipped upon the altars of our society. But all have shown themselves powerless, weak, and destructive, bringing nothing but curses. This is why our nation needs to come back to the heart of faith and begin to call the fire down on the altar of our hearts. Personally, then nationally. This will present a monumental shift that will bring the caliber of resolution that can only be found in Jesus. We can focus our attention on prayer decrees that the Lord has placed in our hearts for this nation that will rekindle the flame of first love in our own hearts and lead into our nation. This will break complacency, blindness, and idolatry off our nation.

Releasing Intercessions Over America by Darlene Curry

Intercessor!!! Almost forty years ago, I found myself in front of this very bold Native American Woman. She shook her slender finger in front of my face and boldly said, "Intercessor! You will be an intercessor to the nation and to the nations." I had no idea what that even meant, and why was she so adamantly pointing me out? I looked around because surely, she must mean someone else. Her gaze was locked on me, and when I looked at her again, she simply said, "You." I weakly said *okay* and walked away, having no idea the impact that this would have on my life. I was just freshly born again, but if it had to do with God, I was definitely hungry for it.

intercession

noun

in· ter· ces· sion ˌin-tər-ˈse-shən[1]

---

[1]   Merriam-Webster Online: https://www.merriam-webster.com/dictionary/intercession

Synonyms of intercession

1: the act of interceding

2: prayer, petition, or entreaty in favor of another

intercessional ˌin-tər-ˈse-sh(ə-)nəl

adjective

intercessor ˌin-tər-ˈse-sər

noun

Not too long after that word was given to me, I seemed to find myself with little ones in tow at pretty much every single prayer meeting that I heard about. I didn't really think about the prophecy or even recognize that it was a prophecy, but it was like I was drawn with gentle cords of love to every prayer meeting that I could get to. I had amazing but super tough, seasoned prayer warriors around me who helped me to learn the power of the Word of God. A supernatural thirst was deposited in me not only to know the word but to let it dwell in me richly.

Let the [spoken] Word of Christ have its home within you [dwelling in your heart and mind—permeating every aspect of your being] as you teach [spiritual things] and admonish and train one another with all wisdom, singing psalms and hymns and spiritual songs with thankfulness in your hearts to God. Whatever you do [no matter what it is] in word or deed, do everything in the name of the Lord Jesus [and in dependence on Him], giving thanks to God the Father through Him. Colossians 3:16–17 (AMP):

I learned early on decree a thing and it will be established! You will also decide and decree a thing, and it will be established for you; And the light [of God's favor] will shine upon your ways.

As a young wife, mother, and convert, I needed all the help and truth that I could get to come in and destroy all the lies that had tried to take me out. God began birthing in me a passion for several three main specific things:

#1. Seeing a generation of youth and young adults absolutely on fire for the presence of God in their lives. Catching fire and becoming contagious!

#2. Seeing people discover why they were created and watching them become free through the finished work of the cross and

#3 A heart cry for the Nation and for Israel but mostly for the East Coast. My heart burned and still burns to see revival w/o end on the East Coast. There are so many ancient wells of revival up and down the coast. In 1857, Jeremiah Lanphier held a prayer meeting that started out slowly but quickly gained momentum and spread like wildfire in New York. Prayer can change the world. Don't take your intercessions lightly. There was a lot of darkness and hopelessness with the stock market crash and great financial uncertainty, but it was the perfect canvas for God to move.

This was the first revival beginning in America with a worldwide impact. From the United States, the revival spread to Ireland, Scotland, Wales, England, Europe, South Africa, India, Australia, and the

Pacific islands. In geographical and proportionate numerical extent, the revival of 1857–1860 has not been equaled. Hunger is contagious, and desperation must be met with MORE. Unlike earlier awakenings, prayer rather than preaching was the main instrument of revival. Tents were often set up as places where people could gather for prayer, introducing a custom followed by later revivalists. No celebrities, just hungry, nameless, faceless people massively in love with the King of glory, who simply love the presence of God more than anything and who carry a ginormous YES in their hearts; people who saw the power of prayer and ferociously went after it.

What if God wanted to use the prayer inside of you to spark a revival fire? What if God wanted to use it to shift a whole culture? Start a movement? What if He just simply loves hearing your voice when you talk to Him?

When things on this Earth seem dark, it is a perfect time to turn on the light. It's a perfect time for prayer and intercession! New spiritual life gets imparted to the dead, and new spiritual health gets imparted to the living. Our God is an all-in-all God. I believe that every move of God is preceded by prayer, intercession, and supplication.

Even well before that outpouring in New York, there was such a rich revival history of Circuit Rider Preachers that would travel many hundreds of miles, sometimes thousands, to reach anyone and everyone with the good news of the gospel. America was Awakening! Signs, wonders, and miracles were being manifested. Hunger drew people from far and wide.

Ordinary people from every station and race were encouraged to make a personal connection with God instead of relying on a minister.

Between 1739 and 1765, George Whitefield preached passionately about the love of God, the reality of sin, and the wonders of heaven!!! He was just one of many that God used mightily in the first great awakening on the Eastern Seaboard, and my passionate desire as an Intercessor was,

"Lord, do it again, but only MORE! A revival with no end and a vast army made up of a generation that would not settle for less than anything but the most from the Most High God!" A radical generation of world changers, walking in the fullness of their God-given identity and design.

I spent much time being face down, on my carpet, crying out for God to sweep our land with a powerful revival with no end! So many of us were crying out for this. We've seen trickles here and there, but there is a tsunami of revival fire that's coming that won't be quenched. I believe the fields are riper for harvest than ever before!!! My heart began also to churn and burn for Israel with great increase and fervor in ways that I didn't understand. I asked the Lord about it, and He simply said,

"I'm giving you My heart. And that's a huge part of intercession. Find out what's on Trinity's heart about a matter and co-labor with God to see it manifest on the Earth. It's a joy to partner with heaven."

God began to send me on wild assignments. I'd need a whole book to tell of them, but it's been a long season of being nth-degree obedient that actually has not ever ended. Go here. Pray over this body of water. Pray over this original seat of government in this town. Take communion here. Soak an oyster shell from the Eastern Shore in salt and oil and await My instructions concerning that (super wild story for another time).

Do a Jericho on the Bay Bridge, Decreeing what I say, and pray up and down the Eastern Seaboard from Maryland to Maine and from Maryland to Florida. Pray for the Eastern Gate of Israel, and at the end of your seventh go-round, blow the trumpet 7x and blow the shofar 7x. Then lift a shout. Before that journey, God had said to me in my secret place, "In 2008, I will open wide the gate. "He had given me a very vivid vision concerning a spiritual gateway about 2/3 of the way when you cross the Bay Bridge.

"I want you to blow a silver trumpet and pray up and down the Eastern seaboard."

I knew right away that it was a heralding trumpet. I said to the Lord, "But I don't have a silver trumpet." That didn't seem to matter a bit to Him at all. I told my team of Intercessors, and we prayed about it for quite some time. God presented that trumpet to me one Sunday through a major "Gatekeeper "assigned to Washington, DC. I shared the vision, and he gave me the trumpet. It was one of the trumpets they used for the Feast of Trumpets. At first, I said, "I can't take your trumpet." His reply to me was, "We need you to have it." Well, there was no wiggling out of the assignment after that. The intercessors and I prayed and asked the Lord when we were to go. On the morning of

02/08/2008, we went. All bridges in America were under high-security alert because of the anthrax scare, and some people were afraid that we might get arrested, but God was absolutely training me that if He said to do something, I could trust that He was with me. I had many wilder and crazy adventures since, then many of them with my wonderful adventurous husband and our kids too, and I would love to tell them all, but I want to skip closer to now.

I absolutely love that my husband Roy is also so wild and radical! We hosted House Church for over twenty-five years so that the youth and young adults would have a safe place to come and worship and encounter the Trinity. We also had tons of prayer meetings, 12,24,48-hours prayer, worship, and fasting meetings. Soaking! Art Community. You name it. We're so grateful because that house was totally dedicated to whatever God wanted to do, and boy, oh boy, was it gloriously wild and beautiful. Secular people would even come into our home and begin weeping uncontrollably. They would be experiencing love and peace. There were tons of angels there, and we were so grateful for all that the Lord allowed us to do. In 2014, we began to travel outside the USA to the mission field and on some awesome prayer assignments!!! I had dreams of missions for what felt like forever, but God, at just the right moment in time, brought them to pass. One of our wildest assignments was Ireland in 2014. We learned some incredible lessons there that would really change our intercessions and the way we would live life.

Daily we would dedicate our day to God and ask Him what was on His heart for the day. What direction do You want us to go? Who do you want to connect us to for Your glory? It's not that we didn't do that before, but this was super intentional and the next level of listening. We knew we were to go to the Valley of Angels (Bangor) and that we were to cry out for revival on the land and re-dig the ancient wells of revival that started back in the days of St. Patrick. But we absolutely need to know what day He wanted us to go. On the morning of Good Friday, we discovered that that was the day. We had been praying for twelve years for this moment, but the timing of the Lord is perfect! We declared that we would dance with the angels after our prayer assignment, and we did. I tried to take a picture of my husband, but I realized after a couple of tries that he was covered in glory. I dropped everything and said, "Here I am, Lord." My prayer during this trip was Lord teach us to live this way in America. Order our every step. May we always hear Your voice saying, "This is the way. Walk in it."

> Your ears will hear a word behind you saying: "This is the way, walk in it. When you turn to the right, or when you turn to the left."

We wanted to be like the wheels within the wheels moving as the Spirit moves.

The trip that would also capture our hearts in such a life-impacting way was when we were fighting against human trafficking in Brazil. We had so many prophetic words for us concerning Brazil, but God made us wait four years before He released us to go. We learned on an even deeper level how He holds time in His hands and that He's trustworthy. No one can thwart His plans, and His plan was for us to go in 2015 filled with His love for all those whom we would encounter. We went again in 2017, and we were so smitten with the land, the people, and the ministry that we were willing to give up everything in America to go and minister in Brazil. When we got home to America. We took several steps of faith. I gave away all my winter clothes, we applied for the paperwork through the Brazilian legal system, and we began downsizing our home in preparation for selling it. Hardest thing ever. So many memories and encounters. During this season of hard work, letting go and listening and praying to know God's will if we were without a doubt called to live and minister in Brazil, was such a time of dying to self and absolute surrender.

Amid our listening and waiting, God gave me a dream. In the dream, Roy and I were driving across the USA in a big RV. Now here's a bit of a back story. Roy, years earlier, wanted to get an RV and sell our home, and I was dead set against it. However, I would talk to God at my kitchen window over some years' time about a desire to see His beauty in all fifty states. I talked with Him often about this. At first, it was all about beautiful forests, majestic mountains, and glorious waterfalls, but it quickly turned to God's beauty through His people. I didn't realize that I was about to see the hand of Jehovah Sneaky move things around in our lives in ways I couldn't even begin to imagine. We were at the time working part-time at a historic Inn on the Eastern Shore. My husband was Mister Fix It, and I was a paid Intercessor. After work one day, we were watching the sun go down on the Bay. I heard myself say to my husband, "I wouldn't mind traveling the USA with you in an RV. He says to me with eyes wide, "Do you really mean that?" I say, "It's so weird, but I think I do."

I had a dream, and in that dream, we were traveling across the USA in an RV. Well, Roy wasted no time at all, and the very next morning, we went to look at RVs. We had the question in our minds, though, and in our prayers, "What about Brazil?" The leader of the ministry that we were going to connect to was soon coming to the States for a much-needed rest. I put a fleece before the Lord. God, if You don't want us to move to Brazil, have them not contact us and let my feelings not be hurt if they don't. Sure enough, no contact until they were back in Brazil. They were considering themselves at that time if they would continue there in ministry. We were pretty sure that we were to travel the USA and pray in every state. Also, at some point when I was sort of pining away over my desire to be back in Brazil, I heard the Lord ask me if I would love America like I loved Brazil. I knew in my heart that I must give myself to what God wanted next, and He wanted prayer and intercession in every state in our country, and He was asking us to do it. But He was also working behind the scenes in the hearts of others to join this worthy cause.

While waiting to hear when and where, I had a dream, and in that dream, I was talking to my dear friends Kim Abbot and Tara from Kentucky. She just happened to be visiting the house where our RV was parked, so that morning, I told her the dream, and she said, "You and Roy must come to Kentucky. We prayed about it, and off we went. That night Kim took us into West Virginia, and I got a vision of Kentucky, West Virginia, and Ohio being on fire with Revival. I knew we had to come back and pray over those lands and the connecting bodies of water. We also visited Cane Ridge Revival Meeting House. There was a mighty move of God there in 1801, and the presence of God and the holiness is still very tangible. I'd given twenty-five years of intercession for the Eastern Seaboard, but I believe God was setting our hearts ablaze to prepare us for what was coming!!! And what I absolutely love about my husband Roy is how nth degree obedient he is to the voice of God. He's a good, good listener. We trust each other's hearts, and both really seek to do the will of God with an excellent spirit. He's always ready for God's adventures, and so am I. We are in one accord.

We really try never to run ahead of God or fall behind Him. We trust His perfect timing.

Enter stage left. There was this lovely fireball of a woman named Audrey. I first connected with her a few years prior in an Intercessory prayer meeting. She sat next to me, and I could just feel the fire. She is so like a giant sponge wanting to soak up every bit of Him. She's a fierce and fearless Intercessor.

Fast forward, she and I had been trying and trying to connect outside of Church, and I think it was in 2020. We finally did just to have time to share and hear each other's hearts, and it was awesome! At the end of our conversation, she said I feel led to share this dream I have with you. I didn't know why at the time, but I had these Holy Ghost chills all up and down my arms and spine. As she shared with me her and her husband's dream to get an RV and do a prayer tour across all fifty states in America, I was absolutely flabbergasted and mind-blown.

189

Wow, God! I shared with her the dream I had and told her that we were waiting for the instructions of the Lord. For a while, people were wondering why it looked like we weren't pursuing what God had told us, but we were listening and watching and waiting.

Our families met together and prayed together to ask God for times, strategies, and provisions. We prayed God gave us all the same date, but our Pastors asked us to delay two weeks. We were not idle. We honored our Pastor's request, and we went to certain places in Washington, DC, which was a total divine appointment. We received a lot of prayers, prophecies, and wise counsel. We prayed in several places there. We sought the Lord as to where and when and prayed in Maryland and Delaware. Every place that we went was divinely set up by God. You could not make up the timing. We hadn't even left the area yet, but how we began to see God move was amazing! To me, the Mauldins are, in so many ways, the superheroes of this great adventure. The poppa works full-time for NASA. We call Kendall the "giant slayer." He is gentle, wise, and a powerful man of God.

The momma homeschools two amazing children that we dub the "Kingly Kidlets."

Those kids have been a huge blessing to us in innumerable ways. We learn just as much from them.

And the mapping strategies that God shows Audrey and Kendall are amazing. We will pray apart and then pray together, and wow... just wow! So far, we have been to twenty-eight states, and God has met us and shown us His heart for each state. It's also wild that in almost every state, we end up meeting historians that are so familiar with the land, the laws, the needs, the people, revival history, etc. God is amazing at connecting the dots. Whether we are praying at a state capitol, an ancient revival well, a church, a historical site, or in the streets with the local people, God always shows up. He shows us where to go and what to pray for, and it is a great honor to say yes to this. We believe with all our hearts that in every place He sends us that He will light the fires of revival.

As an Intercessor, the most fruitful and amazing thing that you can do is to inquire of Him. Ask Him what's on His heart and how you can co-labor with Him to bring Him the most glory! God massively loves America. If you are called to Intercession, please speak life words to your state, region, governmental officials, etc. Can a nation change in a day? The government is on His shoulders, and His increase is no end. We are about to embark on the next leg of our journey, and our passionate desire is to hear and release upon the land all that is in the heart of God for each place. God bless America!

Father, we thank You that You are the faithful and true covenant-keeping God. This nation is dedicated to You, Lord.

> One nation fully **under God**, indivisible, with liberty and justice for all. And I declare in accordance with Your Word "Blessed [fortunate, prosperous, and favored by God] is the nation whose God is the Lord, The people whom He has chosen as His own inheritance."

> Psalm 33:12 (AMP)

Your Word vehemently urges us to make intentional petitions (specific requests), prayers, intercessions (prayers for others in authority) and thanksgivings be offered on behalf of all people, for presidents and every governmental authority and all who are in [positions of] high authority, so that we may live a peaceful and quiet life in all godliness and dignity. who desires all people to be saved and to come to the knowledge and recognition of the [divine] truth.

1 Timothy 2:1–2, 4 (AMP)

Pour out godly wisdom on those in authority and surround them with godly counselors. Infiltrate every governmental office with godly men and women with Your purposes carried in their hearts. May they stand boldly and courageously in the face of evil without backing down one iota from righteousness. Give them eyes to see, and may they have ears to hear God's instruction and eyes to see His strategies for such a time as this.

Father, I pray for true salvation to spread like wildfire across America and the world! Jesus, we declare that Your Blood speaks a better word over this nation. Silence the lies of that foul devil in Jesus' name!

Lord, cause the American people to have a fresh revelation of divine Truth that comes from You and You alone. Awaken your Bride to righteousness in Jesus' name.

Let us be a people driven to prayer, and *Let us pray* as it is still day. Lord, we choose as an act of our will to put on humility as a cloak. We join with You, Jesus, who lives to make intercessions for us, and we pray. Lord, we repent for our wickedness, and we turn away from everything that is not of You. We repent for the Church being silent and for hiding away when You called us to holy boldness. We repent for prayerlessness.

We declare that Your Blood is sufficient to atone for ALL of America's sins, and Your Blood is sufficient to grant America forgiveness for deceitful acts, violence, murder, racism, hatred, abortion, immorality, faithlessness, and betrayals of a sacred trust. Jesus's Blood is more than sufficient. Lord, let this Nation love what You love and hate what You hate and run from all forms of evil. America, Your heritage is unparalleled to any other Nation. Never on the face of the Earth has there been such a country, this wonderful Nation. God, we come into agreement and alignment for everything that You ordained for America, everything in Your heart for America, original intention, and design. Thank You for our founding fathers who were inspired by God and the original inscriptions and documentation over this nation that brought glory to God. Thank You that this Nation was founded on the Word of God and that Word will not return void.

And even as I write this, my heart is warmed because of the revival fire breaking out through college universities, but I cry out for more, MORE LORD. May the fire of revival cover this nation and have global significance once again, Lord.

Let the name of Jesus Christ be lifted up over this nation like never before!

May we be counted a sheep, Nation. Signs, wonders, and miracles as the new normal. Thank You, Lord, for pouring out the Spirit of God on all flesh, and may there be mass deliverances and healings in confirmation of the preaching of the Gospel of Jesus Christ. Holy Spirit, come move in power. Stadiums will fill up with people fasting and praying.

Lord, as there is a massive shift happening in the Earth, let there be such a tsunami of Your love covering this Nation... inescapable love. Ready us, Lord, to disciple a nation. Redeem and restore the family structure back to the original intent, design, and DNA that was in Your Heart, God. I pray for supernatural unity for America. Make us truly the "United States" of America with the heart and desire of God!

Thank You, God, that our tongues are being salted with a desire to know You like never before. Father let holiness grip the US like never before. I decree and declare that we are one nation under God with liberty and justice for all. You're exposing and uprooting all the evil in the land, and the Ruach of God is blowing on every son and daughter to rise and be awakened to who You are and who they are called to be in You. Awaken, Awaken, Awaken, in Jesus' name. Awaken every son and daughter and shake them with Your love, the ones who have had their identity stolen by the evil one. Wrap this young generation in truth and peace, all anxiety and stress, and fear of the future. May there be such boldness. I place a clarion call as a spiritual mother to each and every millennial to come into the fullness of all their God-given destinies and callings.

Holy Spirit, move with power and might across the Land and the world. Expose and eradicate every bit of human trafficking in the land. Thank you, God, for every captive being rescued and ransomed and covered by Your love. Expose all corruption in Government. Thank You, God, for raising Your standard in America.

I thank You, God, for such a mighty move of You that history has ever seen! I speak Your holiness into every sphere of influence. Grip our educational systems with Your truth and let everything not of You be eradicated in Jesus' name. Holy Spirit, sweep clean our educational institutions with the power and glory of God.

May Your holiness and glory fall upon the seven mountains of family, **religion, education, media, entertainment, business, and government**. Eradicate every evil system, faulty belief system, and every world system that would try to eradicate the knowledge of You. We acknowledge our deep need for You in this Nation and the Nations of the Earth. Righteousness and Justice are the foundation of Your throne, and we declare that You reign. In the matchless name of Jesus, I pray. Amen.

- CHAPTER 9 -

THE JOURNEY BEGINS—
TRAVELING THE STATES

Prayer Preparations—Clear Beginnings

After being in the Lord's presence, He breathes into our hearts and releases His love over us in a way that enhances our perspective and enlarges his territory in and through us. After our return from the Toronto revival, we received so much clarity from the Lord that our journey was just about to begin, and we were being called as missionaries into our own nation. The journey that God had called us into required us to take a step of faith and buy an RV and travel to all fifty states in a rally to encourage, minister, intercede and love people along our journey. A release of a call back to God movement, reminding our nation how to come back to its first love, releasing repentance and restoration! The first ten states were covered during summer-fall 2021, and a big portion of half the additional states was visited in spring 2022, with intentions to complete our journey within the next two years leading into 2024.

The book that we found ourselves reading months before our travels began was the book called Binding the Strongman over America and the Nations by Dr. John Benefiel with Melanie Hemry (Benefiel 2020). This book was a great spiritual tool in our readying ourselves by first acknowledging the work that had already been done by generals of the faith who had gone ahead and opened the doors over our nation for restoration through intercessions and actions. The ambassadors who have pioneered the journey ahead documented their partnership and existing covenants with the Lord leading our nation back in towards a pursuit of holiness. We sought our apostle's direction, and after prayer, we all heard that we had a year to prepare for prayer and growth. Our team came to our knees in humility before our God and began to ask Him for His guidance and leading. We journeyed with Him in prayer first. It became a time of deep awakening for our team as we started to pray for our nation and the heart of its people.

We also were shown that revival winds are going to be moving as the weather moves from one area to the next! Just as the wind blows from west to east, we perceived that fire would come over the land as the Word of God is released. Great awakenings are going to hit the west and then move like the wind toward the east! And sweep across the nation, all following the wind of the Holy Spirit. Rain was to be a symbol of cleansing and restoration. As the Lord sends rain over the deserted lands, He will bring with it great renewal! It was remarkable that even the RV which was chosen for us had the name of four winds, which we heard echoed in prophecy that the four winds were going to be converging into high potency of His upspringing wells to glide into every wasteland that needed watering.

We partnered with our remarkable friends, who we call Momma Darlene and Papa Roy, which are the elders of our church at RHLC, and allowed God to fill our plans with his blueprints for our nation, starting with the surrounding regions. This strong couple, introduced in Chapter 8, had carried a vision in their hearts for many years and had already taken the steps in their own obedience to sell all their possessions and move into an RV. They were waiting on God's perfect timing. When we were prompted by the Lord to call them and share our assignment, they about rolled off their chairs and were equally excited as they felt that there was a deep alignment for our paths to cross and become a partnership into the move of God beginning with our families, and our church. We had such a strong covering, and our church had just stepped into an apostolic assignment led by the Lord to grant us access to furthering His territory. We began to pray strongly together as we incorporated our apostolic leaders to make sure we had heard the timing of our start date. It was confirmed by our apostles David and Tracy that we were to take a year in preparation and then be released to travel. This time was a gracious opportunity to pray together and link up our strategic visions until we felt ready spiritually and physically.

I remember one day amid prayer on the altar of the Lord. I was in the front of our church praying and asking God if He could give me a true sign that we were hearing Him correctly, as I had just been questioning if we had the true authority over the entirety of the nation. I had allowed a few comments from various concerned people to enter my heart and caused a bit of uncertainty. In my attempt to gain clarity from God, I had a moment like what I imagine Gideon (Judges 6:1–7) might have had, where he asked the Lord to cause the fleece to be dry and the rest of the ground be moistened by the dew. Then he went as far as asking about the opposite effect of the moisture, just to be sure that he was hearing correctly. In His goodness, the Lord allowed this sign to show forth, and Gideon was reaffirmed, showing that he would have the Lord's leadership and success.

In a similar manner, I, too, was allowed to have a similar revelation as a beautiful, submitted intercessor walked towards me on the altar and spoke very softly and firmly. She said, "The Lord is with you and sends you out, He will be your protection, and He will only send you where He has gone ahead of you. He makes way for this journey to be successful." It was all I needed to hear. I knew then that we had all the blessing needed as it had come from our Father and our ministry leaders, which included our apostles. We had followed His order, and now he was blessing our steps and assignment. It drew me into a ready state that now broke off any evidence of fear or doubt. Perhaps, I even found myself relating with King David, who had been anointed in a hidden place for a journey and assignment that would be later activated as he stepped into his kingly assignment. He knew that God was for him and was not timid when it came to slaying the giants of his time. May our journey continue to be one of great manifestation toward his perfect will and purposes.

There are already so many testimonies of revival, healing, and connections that God is making as the journey continues. More and more signs and expressions of our King are revealed. We will share some of these examples in this chapter. However, more of these encounters will be released in the future. As we travel and continue to appeal to families to join us in prayer and acts towards hearing and obeying the words the Lord is speaking over each individual heart. For things to change in this nation, the sons and daughters of the King need to arise and take their places so that change can begin for America. May we begin to see Jesus' light shine in and through us, as we hear in this scripture, "Arise, shine; For your light has come! And the glory of the LORD is risen upon you" (Isaiah 60:1, NIV).

The Nation's Capital—Washington, DC. Ask, Seek, and Knock!

In July of 2021, we ventured South of Maryland and began our journey to Washington, DC. As we were invited to partake in prayer with intercessions that were in the heart of our nation's capital. It was encouraging to visit a beloved prayer warrior who has been interceding for the nation and its leaders for years. We found ourselves nestled in a quiet haven, right in the middle of the national mall, where only senators and people of political office can go. But, because we were in position and in obedience, the Lord said to us, "Come up here, Come up now!" We were pleasantly surprised that there are set locations where the Lord is being praised and sought day and night. An aroma of fragrance goes up regarding our nation that is an entryway for the blessings to continue to flow like an umbilical cord giving nourishment to an infant. As we first stepped into this haven, we experienced the glory of God's secrets being revealed in a rather exciting nature. I felt like He wanted us to know that many of our leaders in this nation still seek Him while He can be found.

In a similar pursuit from Matthew 7:7, where Jesus said, "Ask and it will be given unto you, seek, and you will find, knock and the door will be opened." All this through prayer and the pursuit of always wanting to have God be at the center of our lives. What a joy to have partaken in prayers over our nation and its leaders. We also received a great commission for protection and guidance, as well as heavenly calibration for each member of our group. A beautiful vision was shared between our group, a picture of our RVs being led by the angels and the columbine of the harvester behind our caravans as we harvest the Lord's fields which are ripe and ready to be gathered. The joy is released along the path of our journey as the children laugh and enjoy the scenery at every location that we drive through. The evidence of His plumb line being set everywhere that we go, to call our nation into its place of right standing under God's power and blood as our covering was being laid out.

The Gate Keeper and the Oil of Joy

In September of 2021, a divine setup was sweet as honey to our souls as we were on assignment leading into Field of The Woods in North Carolina. This Prayer Mountain became an entrance to having FaceTime with Jesus. We arrived in anticipation of climbing the prayer mountain in hopes of viewing the sites from the top of the cliffs. Our neatest surprise lay inside a gift shop as we gathered our group and began to search the shop for treasures and maps. Through discussion, we found out that the shop leader was back and recovering after being gone from COVID. She began to share her journey and told us that she was the gatekeeper of the area. Together we shared testimonies of our travels, and she also shared her faith journey. The Lord prompted her to pull out a flask of precious anointing oil that she held carefully for specific moments, and as she walked and asked if she could pray for us, she mentioned that the oil vile was from the original Azusa Street revival held in CA. As she anointed our heads, we all felt the presence of God awaken us to His revelation of the latter rain and perceived that He was eager to move upon our lives and our nation to bring greater increase. We then went on to the prayer mountain, where we experienced the warmth of Jesus enveloping us in such a tangible way.

After prayer, she gave us our assignment and revealed to us a place that needed to be released by our prayers. This place was a few miles below the mountain and had been a revival spot that had been off the map. In 1896, the Shearer School House was a place where the Holy Spirit had come down upon the hearts of an entire congregation and revival visited Camp Creek, North Carolina. Several of the largest Pentecostal churches can trace their roots back to this revival at the Shearer School House.[16] In 1884, Richard G. Spurling (1810–1891), who was a Baptist preacher, and a few of his friends grew weary of the spiritual condition of their existing church. He went on to bring reconciliation between Baptist, Presbyterian, and Methodist leaders and asked them to join a new church called "Christian Union." Eight leaders stood up in the assembly and joined together. Their emphasis included belief in the New Testament that it was faith in Christ's finished work that brought salvation, as well as every individual has the right to interpret per the leading of the Holy Spirit. They ministered together for ten years over the mountains leading to the revival that would be released in 1896. Many rival denominations had burned down their meeting house as they did not understand the movement of the Holy Spirit. This revival touched many lives, and those mountains are still covered with the Lord's favor and blessing. The union church, which led the movement, eventually became the Church of God and is now a denomination that has seven million members in 178 nations and territories also found across the US.[17]

The example we can learn through this movement is that it is not our job to steady the movement of the Lord's spirit. Instead, it is our pleasure to follow His lead and allow Him to move as He considers appropriate. We released the Lord's power to heal the land and those who had been persecuted for their faith. We spoke peace and took communion over the land and asked the Lord for His desire to be fulfilled for this community and unto the nations. It was incredible to witness what happens when denominations set their doctrinal differences and place their faith in the Lord and His finished work on the cross. The unity that the Father wants us to have across the globe with other denominations will set the tone for the third great awakening to come forth.

A Time of Rest in Canaan, Maine

What's in a name? Perhaps everything. What originally began as the name of the son of Noah, who had been cursed, was eventually called the Land of Promise. Another intricate look at how God can redeem a name and store it as a prize representing his redemption. In the days of Abraham, the land of Canaan had been promised to his seed as a possession from the Lord, and Moses's generation wandered in the desert for forty years, unable to obtain the promise due to their disobedience. It was then later acquired by Joshua, who stepped into leadership after Moses, having spent time under the presence of both Joshua and Caleb, were empowered through faith to reclaim the promised land and lead a generation into their inheritance. As the Israelites regained territory by moving into Canaan, they acquired the blessing that had been set apart for them. They had to exercise their faith and move in great obedience (Joshua 3:1–5).

On September 25–27, 2022, we were led to stay at a place called Canaan, just north of Augusta, Maine. It was by no coincidence that it was during Rosh Hashanah, the Jewish New Year. This is a time of reflection for the year up to date and a time of repentance, bringing all things to the Lord. There is a blowing of the Shofar, which opens the call for repentance. Many wear white clothes symbolizing purity.[18] It was a wonderful time of gathering with our team and seeking the Lord together as we realized that we had now stepped into the mid-point of our state's journey. We were now at state number 25. We found that the number 25 symbolizes "grace upon grace." It is composed of 20 (meaning redemption) and five (grace) or grace multiplied (5x5). "And the Word became fresh and tabernacled among us (and we ourselves beheld His glory, the glory as of the only begotten with the Father), full of grace and truth. And of His fullness, we have all received, and grace for grace. For the law was given through Moses, but grace and truth came through Jesus Christ" (John 1:14, 16–17, HBFV).[19]

We learned so much as the Lord took us to a church that was on fire for His plans and purposes. This church, called Kingdom Life Church, was prophetically a lighthouse on the hill, awakening a generation into the plans and purposes of their calling in Christ. We found out that their intercessors had been part of praying for revival to come upon our nation. As they decreed faith-filled prayers for the Lord to come down and touch our land, there was evidence of a seismic earthquake that shook the land and was felt in Maine's tectonic plates. I believe God was showing them through a gateway of His power that there was coming to a shaking over our nation that required much prayer.

Our children, Enoch and Sophia, took notice that the clouds appeared to be angelic, like wisps of flares, and moved quickly with the wind. Our team witnessed the signs in the clouds and received word from the Lord of the wind of the spirit moving through the north and sweeping all the way down the south of the state. We recollected the memory of a prophecy spoken previously that as it goes with Florida and Maine, so shall it go with the rest of the states as they are forerunner states. This made sense that we would find a remnant after God's heart that was opening the gates for the kingdom to release angelic hosts and empower the saints into their right standing in Christ. This ecclesia was hidden among the crevice of the rock. It was a place where the Lord's goodness was being released over the entrant points of our nation.

I believe there are hidden epicenters where the power of God is to be made known to our nation. A tent peg is stretched outward over new territories as the Lord keeps releasing His beautiful revelation. I believe we will be seeing more come from this beautiful entrance

205

as the intercessors roll out the carpet for the King of Glory to enter our nation again. Our whole country has imprints of the markings from our Fathers' fingerprints. Places of increased visitation and full habitation. Resting pads for the sons of God to find peace. It is from these heightened places of rest that we shall begin to release prayers that will shake every dark place and bring about exposure to restore and heal our nation. We are not just called to enter the promised land as Joshua and Caleb did. We are now called to occupy and begin to build a kingdom infrastructure that will sustain the next generation.

Unity of The Gathering of Tribal Nations in Warrior, Alabama 2023. As our journey continues and we keep touching new ground, our pursuit is after the heart of the Father. In an intriguing venture toward healing and restoration, we moved with God's fire to visit Warrior, Alabama—a hidden gem, nestled in the mountains, where tribal leaders from all over the nation visit a site to commune and seek the restoration of the Lord to draw all men to Him. This ministry has been ongoing for ten-plus years and is now partnering with other similar moves that are ushering in an awakening that is fresh from the realm of heaven. We believe that God is after the heart of the very first Americans who lived in this land prior to all the settlers coming into this nation. Ultimately, we know that unity over all tribal nations will spark a fire unlike any prior known or seen in our nation. It begins with forgiveness from all offenses, both past and present, to step into a future of higher heights destined for our grand nation. The vision God gave our team is to visit the four corners next and pray with those who are already seeking His heart for restoration. More will be written and spoken as you can visit our website to follow our ongoing journey across the United States, www.calledtoshine.org.

- CHAPTER 10 -
AWAKENING A SLEEPING GIANT

When we read the prophecy about Gulliver's Giant over our nation, which was shared by Bob Jones in July 2005 at a conference in Cincinnati, Ohio. We were really surprised by the ways that God began to reveal His rhythm and movement as it pertains to the outpour of revival over our nation. He was showing us that there is a synchronization of the bride, families, churches, and faith groups rising out of their places to move with His Spirit in order to orchestrate an unveiling of the restraints that have held the sleeping giant of revival from standing and taking its steps forward. As we received the invitation and stepped into obedience, we were doing our part to untie the giant of complacency and unbelief as we watched the movement come over the land.

The prophecy describes a giant man that had been sleeping and begins to awaken after thirty-eight long years of being held down. The giant had been captured and tied by little people of little input, who had kept him from escaping. Until he begins to have his restraints undone, one place at a time. He describes seeing his head over Cleveland, OH, over a place called "Jacob's Field." His heart was seen to have a large tent peg over the city of Columbus, Ohio, where they would come to see many wonderful signs, wonders, and miracles that would explode over the whole place like a giant tent.

The giant's reproductive organs were said to have been over Cincinnati, Ohio, as it is going to become a place where the kingdom of God is reproducing under the mighty priestly anointing. Philadelphia, PA, was a place where the left hand was seen, meaning that there was great love and great teachings coming from that state. The giant came to rest in Indianapolis, Indiana, and then, it began to rise. The cords which held it down begin to break like rubber bands being pulled off. The left foot was in Charlotte, North Carolina, where there was a giant television broadcasting its awakening to the world. And his right foot was in Nashville, Tenessee, where great faith was rising. However, as the giant started rising, both of his feet stood up in Atlanta, Georgia, as he began to overtake the South.[20] This prophecy was a vision that we didn't even realize we were following until we started to see more clearly in our leading back through Georgia.

Destroying Demonic Strongholds

During September of 2021, we had the privilege to visit Macon, Georgia, and on our travels, we came to visit with a friend living in this area who is also a very prophetic voice who was under Bob Jones for years. After prayer, our friend sent us to pray over the Native American mounds. We arrived early and came to pray together as we were on a mission to find the highest ground to release our decrees. One of our team members had an incident as they were walking into a cave dwelling and struck their heads so strongly that they had to be taken into the visitor center for first aid. We asked the Lord if we should continue after checking on our teammates, and we decided to move forward.

We walked over and climbed the highest mound, which in the past was used as a ritual ceremonial temple. When we arrived at the top of the mound, we came to a flat top, which had a very crooked trail. Curiosity led me and my husband to walk along the trail with our two children following not far behind, then halfway through, we heard a voice of a man shout from a distance. He said, "Behold I made the path straight, and look how they have gone and made it crooked." As we came closer to him, we could see he was drawing with a pencil over the top of the stairwell. What could he be writing?

Isaiah 1:18 (NKJV):

"Come now, and let us reason together," Says the Lord, "Though your sins are like scarlet, they shall be as white as snow; Though they are red like crimson, they shall be like wool. Then he looked at us and said, "You all should release your decrees and prayers to the North from the Lord's altar."

To the Northwest was the City of Atlanta, and so we faced the city and began to decree our prayers. We spoke against the stronghold over Atlanta, and we released the Lord's presence and His angels to bind up the strongman over the city and to close all the demonic portals that had been opened due to human sacrifice as well as bloodshed. We repented the sins done over the city and over the land of Atlanta. We followed the leadership of the Holy Spirit as we prayed together. The Lord released a beautiful rushing wind, and as we shouted over the mountaintop, we felt His presence go ahead of us. After we finished, we looked over at the man, who minutely looked a bit angelic in his long hair and piercing eyes which squinted as he smiled. Then he said, "Good job. It's finished!" We were a bit amazed by his being there, just at the same time we had arrived, and yet he seemed to know why we were called there in the beginning, almost as if he had a part to play in the middle of this as well.

As we journeyed back together, he spoke to us and said that he had come to know Christ after a long journey of being homeless. He said he took a walk up this mound many times, and this day was very important to him. We prayed with him about his health and life situation. Then, we accompanied him back to the visitor center. He kept asking us to be careful as we were not on the good side of town, and he knew we were taking an Uber back to our RV site, so he asked us to be extra watchful. He even told my husband to sit behind the driver to protect me. Interestingly, we boarded a vehicle that was a young man who appeared to be drinking and driving or under the influence. He took us to his home in a rundown part of town and got off his vehicle and went inside, and left us parked for a few minutes, which is against their protocol. We begin to pray in emergency tongues, asking the Lord for His protection as well as wisdom.

After the young man came back to the vehicle, he was carrying a bottle filled with some liquid. Then, he began to drive us to our camp, which was about thirty minutes South. The spirit of God came over us, and we began to minister to the young man. He began to tear up as he shared his story about his broken relationships. The Lord intervened and brought us all into his embrace. After he dropped us off, we came back to our RV to find a colossal ant pile attacking our home. It appeared that we had angered the ant colony over all of Macon, Ga, as we came back to fight off the stream of millions of ants that had tried to take over. After killing them most of the night, we were able to take off within the next two days. In passing, we came across the city of Atlanta, Ga. I asked the Lord if we could stop there, and He said, "Not yet, but what you have done in Macon will impact the city of Atlanta, and you will see it soon."

A Year of Acceleration

About a month after our return, we received a visit from an apostolic leader who came to our church to minister from Atlanta, Georgia. This leader brought with him teachings about the kingdom that released a new grace over our house. He also taught about the courtroom of heaven and the authority of our priesthood found through Melchizedek's order, through Christ. Then he invited our apostles and a group of us back to Atlanta for a Kings conference. We joined them in Atlanta on October 31, 2021, and were able to witness a remarkable event that took place as many apostolic leaders came together from the nation and this city to pray over the land and the city gates. They each gathered and picked up soil collected from the ground in Atlanta, and each having some held in their hands, spoke into the soil the restoration and healing from the heavenly realm.

The Lord allowed me to witness a glimpse of the standing giant in a vision as he was being awakened and drawn by the hunger of these anointed men and women who were standing in one accord, asking God for revival over their city and land. I kept hearing the Lord's voice speaking into my heart, saying this is that which was spoken of in Gulliver's prophecy, which I gave to my prophet. Thus, I knew we were in a new area when it came to revival, as it was getting ready to be poured out over the nation. I kept hearing God speak powerfully into my heart. You're in a new place as a body. Things have shifted, and you are about to see greater things to come. Everything in our church began to go to the next level, teaching, deliverances, healings, conferences, and the school of ministry.

Current Day Circuit Riders

Interesting fact: Over a series of visiting Virginia and the Carolinas, we began to see that God wanted to highlight the trail of the circuit riders, in particular Bishop Francis Asbury, the founder of Methodism in America. He and thousands more to come preached in small communities across the state on this riding circuit. We visited Camp Welfare in Georgia, which was a historical site used during the Methodist circuit riders. We realized that Asbury may have been one of the founders of this camp meeting. We were so tremendously honored that God would take us here to this Holy ground to speak powerfully to us about an existing movement that He wanted us to come into agreement with, as prayers of the past had released a zeal and passion over the hearts of man to ignite a movement in evangelism in our nation's Eastern mountains. The Lord wanted our team to embrace and take note of those who had gone ahead of us to bring about healing over our nation that would later still be instrumental in drawing many to know Christ! He was speaking to us loudly, that in some ways, we are part of the next wave of modern-day circuit riders.

On August 19, 2021, our team took time to walk around Camp Welfare in Ridgeway, South Carolina. A place where revival began in the 1800s. It's been a place that's seen a lot of prayer for many years. One hundred fifty years of continuous annual meetings brought many hungry Christians to these grounds. It was used as a place of worship, and many families came to stay annually for ten days. Sometimes, the meetings went for longer sessions, and I'm sure some people lived there more regularly. The focal point seemed to be an outdoor sanctuary that had open seating with church pews outside under a covered porch area. Directly surrounding this were tenant homes where campers could stay in huts that were right next to each other. All looked like they had a small space for a kitchen, a bedroom, and a portable restroom. Outside of that was an indoor church building and a cemetery that looked like it, too, was ancient. Established in 1876 for the African Methodist Episcopal Zion Church, it showed the blueprint of some of the revival movements, which were led to commune together for longer weeks as they sought the Lord's presence together in prayer and worship.

For five years now, the land has been re-purchased and does not appear to be used. Our team prayed together outside in the open church amphitheater setting, the dust-weathered benches were a hard sight, but the spiritual atmosphere was still electrifying. When we began to pray, we couldn't help but wonder how many prayers had been released on these grounds non-stop for decades and how many tears were still saturating the soil until the assignment of answered prayer was complete. As a team, our hearts longed to see the full use of this site continue to be openly used for healing, unity, and revival! But even more important than that was for us to see the fruition of the prayers that all came from this place, to see healing over the racial divides that our nation has had wounds that have needed healing for far too long. We prayed for every race and every color as well as every people group. We spoke repentance over the hearts of those who had carried the burdens and pain for generations. We asked the Lord to heal our land and our nation from such areas of division and separation.

We loved that the hundred-row houses represented many families that would come to these camps to pray every year and release revival over the state and country. We pray that this ground will be re-used and many families will be led to Christ on the hills of the South Carolina Mountains!

A Nation Yields Its Heart to the Lord (Asbury University 2023)

On February 17th, 2023, our family ventured off to the University of Asbury during the beginning of a revival movement. We found ourselves face to face with His Holiness as it blanketed a small chapel in a town called Wilmore, Kentucky. As 1,700 hungry worshippers sought the Lord in a place where He could be found. Our union was drawn closer as we were all there to behold and witness a new move upon our land. When we arrived, we were led straight to the University, where one of the original revivals took place in 1970 at the Hughes Auditorium, where regularly occurring services are held Mondays, Wednesdays, and Fridays beginning at 10 a.m. This was fifty-three years after that revival last took place, but on this fine Wednesday morning on February 8th, the chapel session did not end as regularly scheduled. Instead, it kept going as a group of hungry, determined students pressed into the heart of the Father. They repented, prayed, worshipped, and read the Word together. Repeatedly and concurrently, the holiness of God's presence filled this temple. They found themselves surrounded and embraced by His love, peace, and radiance. A sovereign holiness came over that place, and it set many captives free as well as filled many with Christ's light.

As testimonies were shared and service continued, many who were outside heard what was happening, and within a few days, this revival began to draw many to the doorstep of this city. By the time we made it to this location about nine hours from us in Maryland, it had been happening for ten days straight. We arrived on Friday, at about eleven in the evening, and drove directly to the university. We came and found lines that were immensely long despite the freezing weather. The hunger that we saw was extraordinary, as people just waited patiently in line, and many just worshipped right outside the chapel as they joined the live stream that was being projected outside on the front lawn of the chapel. We noticed that the line seemed to be moving quickly, so we waited until they allowed us inside the chapel. We were pretty tired, as traveling with two children can be tiresome, requiring more stops and also creativity to keep everyone happy. The minute we walked in at about 12 a.m., we were greeted by very friendly staff, which I could see were exhausted, but they were still serving with such kindness and love. They led us to the top floor to the farthest balcony away from the stage. The first thing I observed was the peace that filled the whole chapel. I bowed my head and just remained silent as I heard the Holy Spirit speak, "Jesus is Lord"! The sovereign move that was happening in this place was so holy.

It took everything in me to hold back tears, and as I looked over at my husband, he was in tears as well. We worshipped with the harmony of the thousand who were standing around us, and it just felt like a whirlwind of praise went up to the heavens as we were entering His most holy throne. The waves of His presence kept moving through the place, and in a few minutes, I felt completely strengthened again and could have stayed there the whole night. In those moments, my flesh was re-awakened. Having our children with us made us aware that we had to make our way out within the hour to give them rest for the next day to be one of success.

After about four hours of rest, we arose and quickly got ready to spearhead a new day and assignment. We were determined to try to get inside the chapel again to spend time in the Lord's radiance. Our efforts to be there were not fueled by any actual lack or problem in our lives. We just wanted to embrace what he was doing there, now, and witness through submersion in the deity of His goodness. For all my friends that kept commenting, why should I go there if I am already fully awake and alert to God in my life? All I would say to them is my childlike fervor would not allow me to miss out on this once-in-a-lifetime opportunity to witness what the Shekinah could release in an atmosphere where He chose to upwell from both within and above. It was a nestling within His holiness that felt like we could have seen or done anything, an environment impregnated with the possibility of all things being possible. Could this be anywhere if we were standing in Him? Absolutely, but having the burning desire in me to run towards His light caused me to become the firefly drawn to His beacon.

It was about eight hours after the line moved closer, and we enjoyed talking to people around us who were visiting from Ohio, Buffalo, NY, Florida, Canada, and so many more states. We almost didn't make it inside, but as we pressed through, we were able to get in by about 4 p.m. The presence of the Lord was beautiful. Though thousands were surrounding the place, there was no pushing, no arguments, just worship and peace among all His children. We were all one in unity, pressing toward the one we all sought. He filled immesurably us as we came to worship together. As we found our way inside again, it was just enveloped with His oil, as if a mirror was being held up to our hearts inviting us to let Jesus search our inner parts. Yes, our heart was being softened and reset to His plumb line. He began to reveal deep areas that needed to be consecrated. As His fire turned up, all I could do was humble myself and ask Him for more. I wanted to be so clean before Him, and I believe He was already doing the deeper work as our family just sat or stood in worship before Him.

An entire generation of young adults had captured His heart and then was serving others with love and intentionality who were longing for His presence. This was an image of sacrificial love. The beautiful photo in my memories was how the Lord filled them up so that they could then fill everyone around them up with His deep love. This movement led through repentance and has overflowed into many more universities along the nation and even unto the nations. The rolling fire connects us to His Spirit. This union is not something that could be stopped. I believe we are moving into a new season of holy consecration by our Father's divine leading. He is opening the heavens and bathing His sons and daughters in a communion that will leave us filled with His love and peace. Unfortunately, the world's ways have led many into has been suffering mostly because of the poison dripped in by fear, but as the Lord leads, the Lion of Judah raises a new standard. He is rolling out with thunder as His presence touches our lives. There is a reclaiming of reverence and a return taking place. A new generation stands up in great courage to contend for access to the inheritance of a kingdom foretold, and it begins to be unearthed.

- CHAPTER 11 -
COMING BACK TO THE CROSS

Our First Love

It's all about Jesus, as He is the intricate reason why we live and breathe and have our being on this Earth (Acts 17:28). Right now, anything outside of seeking and honoring as well as getting to know Him is nothing more than wasted time. When we come to know that our entire lives have been designed to fully know Him and become His perfect prize, we realize that it's in this place where He is the central point of our adoration and existence. As we seek His kingdom first, we realize that everything else will expand from that place of His love and grace. He directs our hearts and paths into a place of repentance, reconciliation, restoration, and reformation, all through His divine revelation. We learn in Song of Solomon 8:7 that many waters cannot quench love, nor can the floods drown it. If a man would give for love all the wealth of His house, it would be utterly despised. Therefore, we can be secure in the fire of our King's love.

What gets me excited is knowing that He first loved us. Therefore that same love beckons my heart to open to Him and invites me into His perfect relationship (1 John 4:19). His Shekinah light searches our soul and heart and brings us into a place of perfect receiving. This gift of becoming a receiver of all that Jesus gave for us, so we can then turn around and make Him our focal pursuit as well. Yes, He wants to be known by us all. In His prayer in John 17, He spoke to the Father regarding our state. Jesus wanted our eyes to be open to know what this perfect union with the Trinity is like. He asked God to give us a deeper bandwidth to come into this awareness of His love, drawing all creation back to His original intent. We are in Him and are like the fourth man in the furnace, with His Trinity, becoming pressed into one new man (Daniel 3:24–26).

John the Beloved seemed to have it down, as he had come to know his relationship with Jesus was ultimately worth everything. He spent much time knowing that he could come close enough to hear His heart as He reclined next to him. That's the invitation he gives us all in Ephesians 3:19 (NKJV):

> To know the love of Christ which passes knowledge; that
> you may be filled with all the fullness of God.

Kingdom Relationships—Forged in the Presence

Our second visit to Toronto, the Light the Fire Conference on April 2019, became a face-to-face love encounter with Jesus. After revealing His heart in such intricate ways, by speaking volumes over us, it was amazing watching how many prophetic words kept coming our way, and it was all based on His perfect timing and alignments. We met many pastors from various locations that God wanted us to relate to, from the US, Canada, Argentina, and Juarez. I was led by the Spirit of God to interpret for a pastor from Argentina who was filled with the Lord's fire and was being used to encourage the saints. He had served under the ministry of Evangelist Carlos Anaconda, who is a well-known deliverance minister out of Argentina. It was incredible watching such a beautiful prophetic Word flow in union with God's direct power, establishing His Word in the hearts of men and women alike. After interpreting for a few people, this man of God turned around and began to bless my husband through the gift of prophecy. He came over to me as well and said that the gift of faith would bring me to see the most impossible become possible through God. He said the dead shall rise, and restoration shall come forth into the lives of people you stand in faith for, wow! I was immensely blessed by this Word, and it continues to echo into my heart regularly as I continue to pray in these areas for the manifestation of God's power to be released.

Healing Is the Children's Bread

Entire books of revelation from the Word of God were being opened before our eyes and taught by great teachers and preachers over the course of four days. We worshipped the Lord throughout the day and continued receiving His healing in various parts of our bodies. In one session, I was standing in line awaiting the restroom and had been having back aches that had been ongoing for about a year, a woman who appeared to be of Indian descent came toward me and said, "I need to pray for your back." I asked the Lord if this was alright, and He released me to receive from her, so I followed her outside of the restroom. She began to intercede for me in the spirit, and I felt the Lord's presence fully wash through my body. I lay down and felt a heating blanket come over my abdomen. When I looked down at my body, there was nothing on me. Her prayers were firm, bold, and powerful, ignited with so much faith. I immediately felt an adjustment. By the time I stood up again and found my husband in his seat, the house leaders were releasing healing. I began to celebrate as my body and bones were popping and cracking back into place. Tremendous waves of healing came so intensely and transfused me into my Father's wholeness.

The last part of the conference was a final teaching by a humble pastor who simply had us put our eyes solely on Jesus. It was so simple that it almost became a bit offensive to me. I just kept glaring at my husband, saying there has to be more…I knew there was something wrong with this reasoning, as there should never be anything more than Jesus! He has got to be everything first! So many times, this simple example can weed out our journey's first pursuit. Have we sought Him and Him alone? Is He worth more to us than precious gold and diamonds? As I left the conference, in a bit of disappointment, I contemplated; where was the fire, the miracles, the grand finale? It didn't dawn on me until I was in my hotel room when God spoke very clearly and said, "I want you to come back to your first love, Jesus!" I dropped down to my knees as this awareness moved from my mind to my heart and brought me from tears into deep wailing. Father, forgive me if I have made my desire everything that you have to offer. It's about Jesus and nothing else. He is my true heart's desire. To obtain His love and His heart, to be made one with Him, is everything. On our way home from Canada, I wrote the following revelation.

May 5th, 2019

JESUS. It all comes down to this one name! Everything else is just the outflow from the central connection we have to Jesus. Just as the waters begin at His feet, then streams move outward toward His purposes and with the desire to cover all dry ground so that flow may create green pastures. As I'm brought into awareness of His gift of love, it's the starting point for waves to ripple into the river's edges. If a prophet or evangelist enters my life riding a wave of supernatural love, do I try to jump on board their waves and fail to see that I am a wave carrier used as a conduit for God's rivers to be carried in great measures? I am called to begin at the altar of the sacred sanctuary and ask God to open a new river line that I can ride in faith and move further and deeper than I dare think. That I may glide with His Spirit into His eternal rivers to eventually go to areas that have not yet had oil wells dug up. It's all part of pointing back to His goodness! In the same way, I can ride great title waves in prophecy, healing, and even in glory as He gives us all of Himself. But I must never get lost or forget the source of the flow, where it all begins, and where it all comes from! JESUS!

If I don't have my own relationship, I can get lost on the outskirts of His fringes because He is glorious. But at the end of it all, it becomes evident that the sustainment comes from being in connection and beholding the King upon the holy throne. My first love, have I done well by remembering that Jesus is my prize at the end of every encounter! Have I set stones of remembrance to give Jesus all the praise and let Him be glorified with every part of myself? Have I come back after the immense move to accredit that it was not possible to ride any wave if it was not for His goodness? He is the gift; He is the reward! He alone is what matters most! Did I sell everything to follow Him?

Has it always been all about Jesus? He brought me back to the beginning and reminded me of the times when I valued Him before anything or anyone else! When I was so in love that I looked forward to escaping from others' presence and entering into a secret place to bare my heart before Him! He reminded me of my heart's deep cries!

Ecclesiastes 1: everything is foolish-account of chasing the wrong things. I'm undone as His Holy Spirit spoke to me about this in my car leaving Toronto. He gave me the verse then He referenced it! To sum up my encounter! All that matters is Jesus! Did I fall in love with Him, did I meet Him again as though it was the first time, or, better yet, was it even deeper than when I first laid my eyes and heart on Him? I was prepared to receive Him in more depth! All the preparation, all the words, and all the deep cleansing have purposed my heart to receive His presence. He revealed that by saying "yes" and leaning into His love. He peeled off the hardness of my heart so that Jesus could be unveiled, and I could truly behold Him with eyes that seek only Him! Every time I look at Him, He's more glorious!

The waters flow into rivers at the Holy throne of Jesus! They then move outward with pure fire, carrying the holy vibrancy to awaken everything. The further out they go, the deeper they become. More faith arises with every step. He is well pleased. As we come to the end of ourselves, we don't look for our way. We look for His desire in us!

His rivers are much more able to lead us where he best wants to take us! A stream's flow is not in resistance. It doesn't travel like wild upstream trout. It flows easily with wind and gravity, leading downward into a larger conversion point!

If we're trying to go upstream and feel resistance, we've got to ask ourselves, was I following the title wave left by another man? Did I miss the linking point, which brought me back to the source? Are things no longer enjoyable, or do they lack life? It could just be that the presence of Jesus needs to become my central point again! I may need Him to remind me of where it all began! It's time to come back to loving Him and being loved by Him! Dancing with Him again and lying next to His feet just to spend time with Him! It's a season to be a Mary at His feet, not be burdened by the heavy load that we think requires our plows and shears. Yes, there is time for the work as well, and the harvest is truly plentiful. But in this hour, He is speaking heavily over His beloved Bride. Do you understand how good He is as He prepares the way? Are you taking rest in His marvelous presence? We only want to move as He moves, and if He is calling us into deep rest and surrender, then that is exactly what we have got to fight for.

Viewing the World and Our Lives Through His Lens

If there is anything found in us that has filtered our views of the circumstances around us, we must have our lens brought in for calibration or balancing by the Lord's leadership and allow his love to wash us. I heard a story that was of great impact at our last woman's conference as a true worshipper, Kim Abbott, spoke about the lens of our heart and eyes, which, if led by the Lord, can move us forward and help us survive when things seem impossible. The emphasis was made on our lives' outcomes, which can be impacted by how we think and believe about things. Our perspective on the matter or state of things can either help us or hurt us.

Kim told the story of how she had suffered from a fall after she had fallen and hurt her hand and face. She described it as a trial of great magnitude. She had never broken any bones in her body, and in this case, as she used her hand to break her fall, her hand broke and was tremendously painful. Over the years of being a passionate worshipper through song and praise, she has led many into the Lord's throne room of grace. Her gifting of playing piano and worshipping before God through song had to be put on hold while her body was healing. However, this journey only led her deeper into intimacy with her Father, as He was the one taking her hand and knitting her back together perfectly. During the time of restoration, she sought the Lord, and He reinvigorated her with His beauty and strength. Thanks to God, she was fully restored and continues to bring the light of Christ into every environment she steps into. Knowing that she is a kingdom vessel, she moves under such a powerful wave of the Lord's glory. At some point, it is hard to see the struggles people have had to go through to find their fullest identity and strength in Christ, but despite the struggles we endure, it's incredible to see how much oil can come from our lives when we keep the right perspective.

Considering her story, Kim told us about a man who she had heard was accidentally locked into a train car, which had a walk-in refrigerator. As he attempted to call for help, but nobody was around to come to help him, he desperately carved out a message for his family which read, I froze to death. The next day or so, he was discovered inside the refrigerator and had been found frozen solid. The most bizarre finding was that this refrigerator had not been working and had not been connected or turned on. It must have been at about fifty degrees. Thus, he died an unnecessary death, as he had become petrified with fear instead. Sadly, he had accepted a death sentence by believing a lie that eventually drew his whole body into shock, causing real symptoms to occur and bringing him to an early death. So many Christians are receiving similar early death sentences if they do not understand their authority in Christ. Too much ground is being given over to the enemy, and that has got to stop.

As she described, this is just another example of the power of our thinking. It could either create value in our living, or it can deplete our strength and bring us down if it is not a guarded and reconciled area given over to the Lord. As we learn to take our thoughts captive and bring them into obedience under the Word of God, "We demolish arguments and every pretension that sets itself up against the knowledge of God, and we take captive every thought to make it obedient to Christ" (2 Corinthians 10:5, NIV). What a blessing to be a friend of God! This is how my beautiful friend Kim walks. She is teaching many people to come into union with the Lord and to worship Him in spirit and in truth.

What Is Truth?

When Pilot came to interrogate Jesus, he asked a famous question that forever rings in our hearts, "What is truth?" It was after he had conversed with Jesus in John 18:37 (BSB):

> "Then You are a king!" Pilate said. "You say that I am a king," Jesus answered. "For this reason, I was born and have come into the world, to testify to the truth. Everyone who belongs to the truth listens to My voice." "What is truth?" Pilate asked. And having said this, he went out again to the Jews and told them, "I find no basis for a charge against Him. But it is your custom that I release to you one prisoner at the Passover. So then, do you want me to release to you the King of the Jews?

The anchor of our hearts is tied to a very important truth. Have we come to realize what this truth is all about, or might I even say, who is truth? Truth looks like something; amid chaos, it shines in absolute peace. We must know that Christ came for us and chose to give up His life so that we can receive His gift of forgiveness and salvation. He must be revealed to us as our Lord and King. These truths must become the start of our new nature. We have got to learn to view our lives under His perfect umbrella or covenant. His truth and words must become more real than our hurts or failures.

How you view yourself matters and impacts your friendships as well as takes away or adds to your sphere of influence. The love of God needs to be received by every part of your heart and have its way into

229

your entire person. I struggled for quite some time, viewing myself as beautiful. Perhaps it's because of the impact of prolonged scar effects. Wounds that have been carried too long and not dealt with on the right level, both spiritually and physically, can grow callouses. When I was about five years old, I had a terrible fall off a step due to an accident and violently landed face first, busting my upper right lip and never had it properly sealed by stitches, so it healed with a larger scar. It became a part of my lens; I saw myself as less than others and always had this small marking on my right lip, which caused many missed smiles. Perhaps it was just a small thing in the beginning, but over time, it festered to become larger. Eventually, covering my original beauty that God had wanted me to see and carry.

Ultimately, it became a hidden wound, one that I had learned to ignore, but I always attempted to keep it as far away from being noticed as I could. In my adult years, when I began to believe in complete restoration, and I listened to amazing testimonies of people who had scars completely removed, I would pray in such ways asking the Father to clear my scar out completely. I never felt completely whole. It was as if this long-term battle wound was fixed on my self-image and view of myself, no matter how much I tried to shy away from seeing it. The most interesting part is that as I speak with family members about it now, they are surprised as it was never an area they even noticed. It had just been amplified in my own lens and in my own imagination. Something rather small had become a trip-up and a stumbling block in my view of self, causing me to see imperfection as ugly.

It wasn't until one fine evening in 2019 that I went to bed as usual, unknowing that I was about to have a visitation. In the dream, I was taken on an elevator and taken through a few stories. I was greeted by very large beings who were extremely tall and towered over most of the people there. They were there as angelic guides. We went up a few floors, and then, it came to a stop at a certain level. I saw many people coming and going up and down the elevators. Traffic was taking them to higher ground. Some I recognized and others I had never seen before. When I was brought to an awareness that it was my stop, I got out and began to walk around.

I somehow knew that this was an angelic encounter, everything up there was amazing, and the type of communication taking place was done on a mind level. As I was led down a corridor of what felt like an aerodynamic city, I was taken to visit a larger being who was towering in height and looked down at me. I came and stood in front of this large being that looked like it could be female and was draped with beautiful garments covering her head and hung over as in loose form. She had to lean down just to allow me to be at eye level, then, as if only by invitation, I gazed into the large angels' eyes. Quickly, I began to see channels and gears, such as instruments that began to move all of various sizes and shapes, fitting perfectly together, and immediately I was being taken into memories of my past. I saw myself as a child, and I saw the effects of the wounded scar. Snapshots of lost smiles begin to flash before me in various scenarios.

There were many missed moments from the first time I was injured all the way through my school years, and up until I grew to be an adult, I had lost many opportunities to smile. I was held back from obtaining the fullest measure of joy. It was interesting how, in time, there was a progression of feeling broken, and it manifested by ways of not feeling beautiful. After a while, I was jolted back from the series of memories and was again standing before this angelic being as she was massive but gentle. She waited to see my expression as I looked back at her. She leaned down just enough to be at eye contact. Before I could say a word, the angel smiled one of the biggest smiles I had ever seen. Its face went up from one side and all the way to another like a half-moon, rising with the reflection of the sunrise. Wow, what a feeling, sweet exuberance rushed through my entire being. I could feel the joy she released, rushing like a flood of emotion through my heart. In another exchange of the mind, I was told, "Now, you try it"! I immediately lifted my smile from ear to ear, and in a similar manner, my whole face had been lit up, with a smile that was bigger than life coming from my soul to my face. It passed through all of me, and I received every smile back from the beginning of the first loss to the existing moment. It was fuller than anything of natural gain and represented an enlargement in my expression. I was able to love deeper and receive greater love. Love and respect for myself, and it came with much gratitude. I kept smiling, and nothing could stop this reclaiming ground.

I was then celebrated by many who were there standing around watching what was happening. Wonderfully for one whole minute, everyone stopped what they were doing, and all focused their attention to validate that I was restored, and their excitement was beautiful. What a glorious sight it was, friends new and old just gathered around me and consoled my heart. It really was a magnificent experience. Then they told me it was time to head back, and another helper came along and took me back to the elevator, where I stepped in and was delivered back to my resting place. That was when I awakened! The most significant reward was that I had so much joy as I jumped out of bed and ran downstairs just to share my encounter with my husband. When I shared it, it was like tears of freedom came rushing through me as I told him I have been healed. I could see myself through the lens of the Father, and there was so much beauty in how He viewed me!

Perhaps there have been areas of imperfection been needing the Father's touch. I pray that He will visit you in your dreams and share with you His viewpoint from heaven so that you are able to hold a glimpse of just how perfect you really are in His eyes. Also, I pray that you will be given the gift of seeing yourself through the lens of His love. Intricate and woven perfectly together by His touch. As the Lord continues to put His hands into the clay that He is molding and brings it into perfect shape. That you would not step one foot off the potter's wheel but hold your feet to the flame and allow Him to have His perfect way made in you. That's the love of our Father. He is willing to work with us, despite our broken pieces and despite our hardened state. Only He can bring us back to a formable slate and oil us with His joy to make us into something fearsome, validated, and ready for His service.

One Baptism—Love Baptism

There are seven different baptisms mentioned in the Old and New Testaments of the Bible, and one is referred to as the One Baptism.

These baptisms include baptisms of Moses (1 Corinthian 10:1–4), baptism of John preparing the way (Mark 1:4–8), baptism of suffering (Mark 10 38–39), Christ baptism (Matthew 3:13–17), baptism of Fire (Matthew 3:11–12), baptism of the Holy Spirit (Matthew 3:11–12), baptism into the name of Jesus (Acts 2:36–38).[21] This last account into Christ's name refers to our receiving his forgiveness of our sins by receiving what He did on the cross, all of Him for all of us. In Romans 6:1–6 (NKJV), it describes that our old self dies, and we are buried with Him, then brought into resurrection with Christ in His perfect risen form. We must receive his life for ours, and we must allow His blood to wash away our sins. As we step into Christ and step into submersion, we become a new creation. This is the path that Ephesians describes below as the One Baptism.

The one baptism is an instruction to obedience, as it is found in Ephesians 4. There *is* one body and one Spirit, just as you were called in one hope of your calling; one Lord, one faith, one baptism; one God and Father of all, who *is* above all, and through all, and in you all (NKJV). The most intense way of experiencing God's radiant presence is to receive His gift through water baptism into His name by His blood, resurrection, and new life in Christ. I thought I had received plenty of His love until He came upon me in a greater way that left me overflowing with bursting emotion as well as fully satisfied by His touch. How can anyone know that they have ever been in lack of a thing unless they experience what fullness in Christ's taste is like?

When my husband, Kendall, and I lived in California as newlyweds, and we both were employed by great jobs, we would take our weekends to visit the surrounding locations and explore the beauty of the western coast. We enjoyed fine cuisine and loved making sure we explored the sights through our five senses. At times of celebration, during our anniversary and other special holidays, we found exquisite restaurants that were top-rated and had chefs who prepared full-course meals. It was heavenly when our taste palate would take in the masterpiece, compiled of the perfect cut of meat, spice, and ingredients that paired impeccably to make a tasty, in-depth creation. It was, at times, so satisfying that we would make sounds as we took the fork and placed the delicious bite of entrée into our mouths. What splendor and joy came over us as we just smiled at the journey of how a delightful meal could bring us into such a euphoric place and grant us entrance into an expression of gratitude beyond our imaginations. The thoughts that came in that moment were how could this even be true, when using just simple ingredients like chicken or fish, how could pairing them up with the right seasoning and spices make such a delightful gift that had always been around, just not yet discovered. I thought I knew what delightful food was like until I tasted the best which was developed through trial and test.

In a similar way, all the time that had been spent in God's presence through worship and praise, as well as laying on His altar, allowing His fire to stretch and refine my wineskin, had brought about a greater heart enlargement. My heart had been prepared for the receiving of His perfect love. In all the time that I had been calling out for more of His presence, He had been preparing my heart to be able to receive more. At a time of ministry, as I was listening to our pastor minister about God's perfect LOVE. Like a flowing river, Holy Spirit suddenly walked right over and walked into me. Yes, right into my heart. I became aware that Love is baptism and could pour radiantly upon our hearts in a manner that will invigorate every part of us. I felt an oil-like substance, which could only be described like hot wax or hot honey just drip from my head to my body and into my heart. The Lord's deep acceptance and comfort wrapped around my whole soul; nothing was left uncovered. I was fully embraced by Lord Himself. Tears came rushing out of my eyes as I could not contain the absolute rushing gratitude for Jesus's sacrifice on the cross.

The weeping did not end for at least six months on and off and came in waves. At times, I would be sitting at my table sipping on a mug of coffee or tea, and an immense flow of that love would catapult me back into a place of such deep revelation of his perfect, applicable, merciful love. What could one do with such an immense gift but share it with the world? That's exactly why the Lord gave it all through His Holy Spirit, as it was intended to bring into the hearts of so many who have suffered and gone astray or just stopped feeling anything altogether. We were initially created to know Him and to experience His love in great measure. At this point in my life, I was just coming to a deep understanding of knowing just how much my Father loves me.

I could say that, in that moment, I felt just like John the Beloved in John 21:7 when he spoke to the disciples and said I am surely His favorite as He loves me dearly. He had learned to open his heart up to a place where he could feel and experience the love of Jesus in such a deeply intimate way it became His gift. He had learned that staying next to Jesus was His great reward, and he was the only disciple that followed Jesus so far as to be a witness of His crucifixion. Then became the first to arrive at His resurrection to witness the incredible knitting together of a perfect, risen Christ. John had the lens of love, which unveiled Him to be a witness to the revelation of Jesus in heaven, emboldened and wrapped in all His power and glory. What tremendous doors are available if we take up the Love that Christ paid for us to receive!

How do we become good receivers of that perfect gift? The love of God must become our hearts' pursuit; we should not just serve and give from a place of expectancy, or else it could turn into legalism. The place from where we can give must come from an overflow to be giving of the right heart. The best part is it's fully available to us all, as He first gave us all of Himself through Jesus Christ. His life for ours. He always had us in mind as it was for us that He came to live on this Earth and to redeem our initial purpose and intent. As we receive Jesus and marvel at what He accomplished on the cross as His blood was poured out for our sins, we repent and turn from our wicked ways, and we draw near to Him. Then we acknowledge through His resurrection that He was raised to life and is seated at the right hand of God; we must partner in the revelation that we are truly one with Him and that finished work is already released in all its intended love. We receive by faith that loves gift, and we are aware of how intimate that love gift has always been towards us. It then springs out of us like a living flowing river set to water the land and people around us and brings everything back to life.

The reality is that we always have been one with Him, He never walked away from any of us, and He is looking to draw our attention to the reality that there is nothing that can ever separate us from His love. It's always been covering us even when we have failed to see its existence. So, when we are open and willing to humble ourselves and allow His Spirit to overshadow us, to shine in His radiance, we can see and experience that love again. It's at this moment that the lies are exposed and put out, we truly find our acceptance, and the old mindsets tied to an orphan upbringing are severed. We've always been the benefactors of the greatest promises made to all mankind.

A beautiful example can be seen in the story of Naaman in 2 Kings 5, who obeyed the Word of God given by prophet Elisha when he was commanded to go wash in the Jordan to have freedom from Leprosy. Though he did not understand or agree with the assignment, he partnered with faith and trusted God. Rinsing himself seven times, he came out the final time fully cleansed. Love will call us to follow Jesus in all measures. It will bring us to the river's edge to receive our sight so that we can begin to take higher ground. It will bring us into a baptism of a new level, one in faith. Our nation needs a love baptism to spread across every culture and denomination.

Adoption into Sonship—Generational Wounds Healed

What an orphan does not yet know is that there is a place of rest called home in Christ. I roamed for quite some time under the deception that I was an orphan on this Earth. I had experienced rejection that had wounded my heart. We grew up traditional Catholics, and our whole community had been part of the same religion for generations. Memories of artistic painting with the stations of the cross surrounding the walls of the old wooden church. Stained glass windows and images of a messiah that was bruised and beaten, unto death and resurrection. Unfortunately, He was so far away, as many internal dialogues I had with these images of Christ, asking, "Where are you, Jesus?" Learning obedience was key, as knowing our time to sit and stand in accordance with what time it was in the church program. Silence was expected of us children as we were taught to listen carefully and be attentive to serving in specific areas.

In 1988, our family was called by the Lord to begin attending a non-denominational Christian church that was functioning under the gifts of the spirit and held offices in the five-fold ministry, we were suddenly invited into a deeper relationship with Christ as our daily Father and Mentor. It was during this time that we received the gift of the Holy Spirit. The extension of our understanding in reading His Word and coming close to Him became a daily opportunity and one invigorated by His Spirit. However, on the opposite end, our close community had grown distant. It was a silent shunning, and some remarked ideas, such as your family has lost its way and inheritance. As they did not understand the transition of change in our journey, as we were being called out of religion and into a relationship with Christ. I still have memories at about ten years old of getting on the school bus and having the children around us call us holy rollers or alleluias. This caused insecurities in my view of the community. However, we did know with such a reassurance that we were venturing into the new spiritual ground by the Lord's leading. And it was simply our job to love them where they were at.

Over the years, I came to find sonship under Christ's love, which was beautiful and life-changing. I knew how much acceptance and love were present in my Father's presence. This adoption into Christ's unhindered love brought my soul into such a bridal union with Christ into His righteousness. And instead of believing the lies of misplacement or disunity, I started to walk in my identity as His beloved. On January 2021, I visited my grandmother, Gloria, for the very last time. I spent a week with her in the Santa Fe mountains as she was ill and preparing for her return to heaven. I spent much time loving her and reading the Word, as well as praying with her. She had gotten sick with COVID and was now ninety-four years old. I knew that I was there to make her as comfortable as I could, and I was also praying for full healing and restoration. She had prepared her heart, and on her last days, I felt the warmth of God settle over her room like a heavy blanket. The soothing warmth of God's Shekinah presence was all over her room and her home.

As she transitioned home, there was a final peace that came over her and the entire room. All her sons and daughters were able to partake of her crossover into heaven. It was a deep moment of healing and restoration. The Lord moved in and began to repair any severe heart issues. I began under the glory of his light to repent of holding any unforgiveness towards all family members, it was humbling, but I knew it needed to happen for my own sake and those who were witnesses. I released any hurts from a time of feeling severed or orphaned by any of their actions, including my own. I refused to allow religious lines to serve as a separation from our union as a family under Christ's anointing. The heavenly hosts witnessed as the Lord began a tremendous washing that followed as all brothers and sisters came together and loved Grandma and each other. We formed a reunion unlike any of its kind, as our love and appreciation of Grandma reflected a spiritual connection of kingdom magnitude.

Across our nation and throughout religious denominations, we have got to stop allowing walls of separation to sever the love of God that needs to be demonstrated to a lost and dying world. There are so many people who carry rejection from certain experiences they have had with various denominations. All the while, God can use anyone despite their religious background. We have got to build unity across denominations and allow God to move through the message of Christ's love and His kingdom first. If we truly get to understand His heart, we will stop trying to build empires and instead reach the lost through the simple love message of Christ. He has made a way so that all people can come to Him and receive His tremendous love. Sonship is for all who would respond to His call. We need to drop our religious mindsets and stop labeling His vessels as orphaned or rejects. We learn that we are to find unity in faith as we also become mature in Christ, as written in Ephesians 4:11–13 (NIV):

> So Christ himself gave the apostles, the prophets, the
> evangelists, the pastors and teachers, to equip his people
> for works of service, so that the body of Christ may be built

up until we all reach unity in the faith and in the knowledge of the Son of God and become mature, attaining to the whole measure of the fullness of Christ.

Prayer: Lord, release us from generational curses and release Your blessing over our families. May our bloodline be cleansed to right standing under Christ's blood. Remove us religious mindsets that attempt to cast a veil over our eyes so that we can begin to see the freedom that Christ paid for to allow us access to His presence again. We release unity over the church body to see each other as one bride in Christ. Dissolve the separation walls that cause conflict between denominations and bring a restoration to have us see each other through the lens of our Father's love. Release us of any rejection and restore our hearts to sonship. Amen!

- Chapter 12 -

THE RAIN RETURNS

I come back to the description of the book of Hosea in Chapter 6 (NKJV), as the remaining call is released for repentance. Verse 1 through 3 reads: "Come and let us return to the Lord; for He has torn, but He will heal us; He has stricken, but He will bind us up. After two days, he will revive us; On the third day, He will raise us up, that we may live in His sight." Let us know. Let us pursue the knowledge of the Lord. His going forth is established as the morning; He will come to us like the rain, like the latter and former rain to the Earth. As we draw close to Him while He can be found, He is quick to draw near to us. May our nation's heart be led into repentance and stay humble in every area. We need restoration on a higher level. It shall come as we submit our ways to our Father and seek first His kingdom above all else. Just as we read to the finals of Chapter 14, we hear of the restoration of Israel, that to me, has become a clear invitation from the Lord saying to our nation, "Return to me, and I will restore your lands and heal all oppression."

The love that Christ releases over us must become who we are in Him, His perfect love for others. Every fear that in the past kept us from the prize must be dissolved as the perfect love of God heals us from the fear of man. A pressing of the olives must bring forth the purest oil in our lives so that we can walk with ease into the areas He is calling us towards. This is the hour to take our places and rise above the current standards. We are not led by existing models. We are to build new molds and be led by the Holy Spirit so that what we put our hands and feet, too, are truly kingdom models.

The Vision of the Mountain Bursting Forth

Dreams have a way of speaking to us through the perspective of the Father's heart and engaging with us so that we can see the impossible things becoming possible. It becomes an imprint of a realm or area in heaven that wants to be grafted into this Earth. As I began this book with a dream, I felt it appropriate to end this final chapter with a few dream visions as only seem right.

The auditorium was filled with a large crowd of people that had all come from many walks of life, each one with a purpose, a desire to see the great evangelist move under the Lord's anointing. The expectation was high as word had traveled far and wide about this minister of the gospel that moved under much authority and power. After so many people had been healed of lifelong illnesses, news traveled far and wide. Everyone there carried the hope in their hearts that they would receive the breakthrough, healing, miracle, or love that they were seeking. We watched and listened carefully to the message He carried. He emphasized the power of the Cross and the Blood of Jesus, simple yet profound truths. Foundational teachings that carried the wholeness that had been missed for far too long. After he was done teaching, our faith had been springboarded to a new level. I stood in line for hours as the renowned evangelist allowed a line to form to go forward and receive the laying on of hands. He was going to release a blessing as he prepared to pray for people. The line was so long that I stood there looking forward as I was at the very back, it felt like it took hours, standing and waiting until I finally moved up to where the evangelist was ready, and as I glanced up and made eye contact, he looked exhausted at that point he had been standing and praying for hours. So, as I got next to him, I asked him if I could pray for him, as it occurred to me that he, too, had needs. He nodded as I placed my hand on his shoulder. Immediately, I was jolted out of my body and into a vision.

A large dove flew beneath me and swept me off the ground. I was ascending to the mountain tops, and I could see the range above the skyline that lay ahead near a desert landscape. It was exhilarating as the wind passed through my hair, I squinted my eyes just to see ahead, but the sheer power of the bird held me in place as His wings spread with great swooping strides along the ridges. An inner voice spoke to me clearly and said look upon the Mountain top. *"Fix your gaze upon that peak."* So, I focused my lens on the highest point and noticed that the mountain was heavily shaking, as in a fierce rattling. It reminded me of a woman going into labor, the violent pain before birth. This verse entered my heart, Romans 8:22 (ESV): "For we know that the whole creation has been groaning together in the pains of childbirth until now."

Great anticipation filled my heart as I watched the peak shake with a violent uproar, a certainty came over me, and I knew that this

Mountain was about to blow its top. I was witnessing a great eruption, but what was on the inside, I wondered? A fear came over me as many questions filled my mind, should I be this close to a volcano? Why would the Spirit bring me here if he knew this was about to break forth? At the same time, I felt a warm love cover me, reassuring me that I was not alone. Things were going to be alright. I held on to the feathers, which were soft, and the warmth of the great dove as I knew that something about His job involved protecting me. He was my comforter and my greatest protector.

Again, a voice in my heart came through with more intensity. I knew there was an urgency as words repeated, "*Keep* your eye on the Mountain. *Watch* closely!" I just fixed my eyes with all my efforts and focused solely on that upper existent of the range, it forcefully blew its top, and rocks just burst in every direction. We glided away, and I saw that what came out was a burst of glistening water that shot up like a glacier. We moved quickly through the air and came along the water as it poured down like multiple rivers and then covered the face and formed ravines going to the lower parts of the desert grounds. As the water touched the dry sand, immediately there was new life springing forth, like instantly watching a tree grow to its full maturing and shrubs, grass, and foliage coming into season. I felt like I was in a Narnia movie, as this supernatural occurrence kept moving around me, and all the deserted places were no longer sparse. They were becoming beautiful oases where life could now flourish. It was breathtaking as I watched life come back and fill everything. Again it dawned on me that things were being restored as to their original intentions in the Garden of Eden.

I was then jolted back into the dream and stood again right in front of the Evangelist, who stared at me, intrigued by my expression. He shouted in a fitting Jewish accent, "Young lady, you have just had a vision. Everything you saw shall come to pass at its set time!" Within an instant, I awakened from this dream and jumped out of bed, ran downstairs, and immediately shared this dream/vision experience with my husband. The feeling that came upon me as I shared this dream was invigorating. It felt as though God left so much memory of it in me that my whole body was still marveling at the vibrations that this dream now felt like a real testimony.

Later that same year, the Lord encouraged me to share the dream with couples struggling to have children. I would retell this dream occurrence to friends that really wanted to have their wombs healed and have things brought back to life, God would bring those to my attention, and I would share this dream. They would receive impartations. One guy that we prayed for at our church was seeking a wife and wanted to get married. Prophetically we decreed that he would find a wife that same year. We got to witness the fruition of that prayer and were also invited to attend his beautiful ceremony for an amazing young virtuous woman who had been prepared just for him. On another occasion during my visits to Africa, I was honored to pray for a friend's wife, who had wanted to give birth to another child. After sharing the testimony from above, I released the grace of God over her womb. A year later, she and her husband messaged us with great news, they had become pregnant, and she was on her way to deliver a beautiful baby boy. Wow, what an amazing God we serve. He can bring all things back to their original intent and give access to healing virtues that have already been released but just need to be connected too. He sure is amazing. All honor to King Jesus.

Niagara Falls

After driving back from Toronto those two years in a row, where God was able to light our fire again, my husband Kendall and I kept having the vision of a Niagara size waterfall pouring over our nation. I knew in my heart that God was preparing us for what was to come soon over our land and our nation. A great shaking had to happen before there was a glistening release of breakthrough, just like the pangs of childbirth that mothers go through. Nothing easy about giving birth to a new life, every ounce of energy goes into the preparation for receiving that child ahead of time, and home is brought into order. The nesting phase allows for self-reflection, setting things into place, and moving old things out of our homes. The nesting season over us has allowed us to reflect on the altars of our hearts, where we daily make our exchanges with the Lord. We already had to endure such a traumatic shaking, which really stunned much of the church, but it also served the grand purpose of bringing us into an awake state. We may have been aware of the slow fade as evil has pursued the heart of our nation, but now we are seeing the agendas that have crept in as they are in full character, debuting their theatrical plots. We can no longer just watch from the outside. It's time to take a stand. As we take our places, we must begin to reclaim our heavenly authority.

Many are watching the clock and trying to get quick results. Many are too distracted to take the extra time to just go a few blocks further to then be able to encounter him deeply. The Holy Spirit ministered to my heart about many who have been praying for the Spirit to come down and have not made any effort to step out of their comforts into an invitation to become the movement he is flowing through. The song I heard, "Open the floodgates of heaven, let it rain!" What has already been pouring out since Pentecost needs to be proclaimed by those who have the sight to see at this hour. Instead of calling down the rains from above, we need to proclaim the truth. Living waters are bursting forth from within. They are all around you. It's an awareness that the body needs. We need to begin to tell them that it is raining and MORE to come! As his sons and daughters, we were called to run out and awaken the church. Every action we take must mirror his heart for our nation and its people. A call into spiritual alignment under Christ's plumb line. It's time to speak what you see in the spiritual realm and begin to see it manifest upon this Earth! There's nothing wrong with asking for the rain, but we have got to also realize that after we ask, it requires a stance of receiving by faith. That is how we start to step into our inheritance for revival and a great outpouring!

> Seek the LORD while He may be found. Call upon Him while He is near. Let the wicked forsake his way, And the unrighteous man his thoughts; Let him return to the LORD, And He will have mercy on him; And to our God, For He

will abundantly pardon. "For My thoughts are not your thoughts, nor are your ways My ways," says the LORD. "For as the heavens are higher than the earth, so are My ways higher than your ways, And My thoughts than your thoughts. "For as the rain comes down, and the snow from heaven, And do not return there, But water the earth, And make it bring forth and bud, That it may give seed to the sower And bread to the eater, So shall My word be that goes forth from My mouth; It shall not return to Me void, But it shall accomplish what I please, And it shall prosper in the thing for which I sent it. "For you shall go out with joy And be led out with peace; The mountains and the hills Shall break forth into singing before you, And all the trees of the field shall clap their hands. Instead of the thorn shall come up the cypress tree, and instead of the brier shall come up the myrtle tree; And it shall be to the LORD for a name, for an everlasting sign that shall not be cut off."

Isaiah 55:6–13 (NKJV)

The One New Man

I happened to witness a conversation between Jesus and the Holy Spirit in my dream as they were partaking of a very intense conversation about an abundant blessing available to us that we have not yet fully obtained. In this dream, I was walking down a corridor, and as I passed by a door that was closed, I could hear two voices talking, and as I paused next to the door, it began to open gradually. I found myself looking into the room and listening to Jesus speaking; at first, I didn't know who the other person was until further revelation came. But as I stood there listening, I heard them talking about the abundance found in this area of prayer and life as if it was a hidden treasure.

When suddenly, they both paused and looked back toward me, then I gradually became conflicted by their holiness, they stared into my heart, and I felt like an unclean being amid their beautiful radiance. I wanted to fall to my knees as something kept me held up. I knew that I needed their approval to stand there, so Jesus said, "It's okay. You are alright to stay and listen." Then I heard Holy Spirit say, "There is a great blessing available to the ones who are willing and constantly interceding for the nation of Israel and all the Jewish people. A blessing so large that they will need help to store it if they keep praying for the Lord's people." I understood then that if Jews and Gentiles prayed for the salvation of all the Jews and the healing over the unity of the bride in Christ, there would be a release of blessings so large that they would need storehouses to hold them. As spoken to Abraham so clearly in Genesis 12:3 (BSB):

> I will make you into a great nation, and I will bless you; I will make your name great, so that you will be a blessing. I will bless those who bless you and curse those who curse you; and all the families of the earth will be blessed through you.

My heart was captured and convicted as I began to confess before the Lord and as I asked Him for forgiveness for not praying more regularly for Israel or Jerusalem as the Lord had commanded. As in Psalm 25:22: "Redeem Israel out of all their troubles." Isaiah 45:13:

"Raise them up in righteousness and direct all their ways."[22] I knew that if the Lord had written scriptures about the apple of His eye, He wanted us to also keep our prayers wrapped around His nation Israel. I then awakened and began to write things down.

It was only a couple of weeks after this dream that I remember hearing about the restoration of Jerusalem becoming the capital of Israel again, and on March 25, 2019, under the presidency of Donald Trump, Israel, and the United States were unified under a God plan. For once again, courage was demonstrated at a great level, as a leader not only through words but in action, followed through on a faith conviction that brought prophecy into acceleration. Our nation stood with Israel, and the blessings of rebuilding and restoration were quickly being manifested under this leadership. A great example of when we become all about our Father's business, he is so pleased that he begins to release the blessings over our nation, its people, and its economy. There are greater blessings ahead as we keep praying and unifying our direction to stand with Israel again. How do I know this? Well, the Lord will defend His beloved nation until He returns. Through the Jewish people, we have been able to receive the Abrahamic, Mosaic, and New Covenants.

Abrahamic—the blessing of the seed of Abraham;

Mosaic—revelation of the laws given to Moses drawing us to repentance and to Christ, and, of course, the new covenant where His laws are written in our hearts, and the spirit lives within us.

A Dream I Have Seen (Inspired Prophetic Poem)

I have a dream that those things we've been praying for are getting ready to be seen. As intercessions have gone forth, the bowls in heaven are starting to lean. Bringing forward a generation of God-fearing, spirit-chasing, dead-raising, faith-lifting, unhindered, pure fire carriers!

I have a dream that America will once again be a nation that is united! It will seek the hand of God again to bring it into a place undivided. They will stand strong against injustice and resist evils. As their hearts will be made of flesh again strengthened to new levels.

This nation will see a great light as an awakening draws them out of their plight. The truth will come upon us, removing the cloud, emerging as we rise from every fear, anxious thought, and doubt.

I have a dream that identities will be restored and revealed. For in their hearts, the Word of God is now being written and concealed. They will run out to every corner seeking who may come to the banquet hall. For in the last hour, the King has made up His mind to release an invitation to all!

His grace will go ahead as doors swing open. His love will be the warm embrace that they receive as they enter the gates that they are led to find. As they prepare, all He's hoping for is that they put on His white garments. They've already been purchased and are adorned with gems of every kind.

I have a dream that we will see a priesthood who's been worshiping day and night. They will step up into a new order, one of Melchizedek's *right.* As they speak from a place of order, the kingdom will flood the Earth with angelic hosts to guard her nation's borders.

A time when men and women will look around and see that next to them stands another human being. Not another color, not another race, but a child of God shining in His grace. All share the same bloodline, measuring red. All are leaning in together as they seek to be fed by His Word.

I have a dream that many will be brought into unity with God's divine peace. Their willingness to submit to Holy Spirit's guidance will bring abundant release! Heavenly gifts in exchange for their ashes. Joy will abound as they dance around in colorful sashes!

Can you hear the liberty bell ringing? As one in faith stands up to free the captives! An echo of songs that their children are singing. Praising and giving thanks to God for His righteous motives!

I have a dream that babies in the womb will be given a chance to live. Each one will witness a greeting into this world of people who love and choose them. Women and children will be safe as a generation rises against human trafficking. No exploitation of the weak as the strong hand of God is rising!

The media will bend knee to the truth, despite its cost or price. The agenda of political strategists will no longer entice. People's hunger for justice and truth will be loosed. As they yearn to honor others, the most wonderful fruits are produced.

I see a generation that prays for its government and leaders. Trusting God could use anyone He sees fit. Praying He exposes all the lies. And standing next to the nation Israel which is the apple of God's eye.

I have a dream that as the prophets line up to speak. We will see sweeping winds enter in and power lift the words into waves of action! I see angels lining the skies as they gain momentum against demonic traction.

Great miracles are being seen again in churches. As they teach the whole Word and not just the surface. Revival is being poured out as God's children are letting out a new sound! One that has never been heard but is coming from another realm!

I have a dream that I can feel now. I can see it now! It's no longer one I'm waiting for, but it's coming forth and being given out to a nation! It's a dream that I can see! It's a faith that I can agree with. It's offered to both you and me.

Let's take a stand and decree this. Let heaven now write this down! We agree with everything that was paid for on Calvary! It was for us and for our nation. As we return and remain united again under God, He makes way for us and establishes our nation upon His Word. He restores, heals, and draws us back as nations under His abode! AMEN!

Let us pray:

Father God, we ask You to draw your nation into healing and restoration, bring peace to Jerusalem, and put all her enemies under her feet. May Your name be proclaimed on the mountain tops, and may salvation come upon the land that You so love. Jesus, let Israel be to You a name of praise. Proclaim all the good You do for them. Restore everything that has been taken away from them, and bring back the goodness and prosperity over the land again. Draw a union between Jew and Gentile so that together they may proclaim Your goodness over all the nations. Bring about a restoring love like that found in the book of Ruth, where redemption came through Boaz and reconciled Ruth even if she was not of a Jewish upbringing. Bring a restoration as they commune over the body and Blood of Christ, reconciled under one love and union. May generations be blessed because of this great love of brothers and sisters uniting as one bride unto Christ's Love.

May the Lord release His great power concerning our circumstances and bring our nation into a place of redemption. Bring out the gold in this nation, which had its original motives set upon you, Lord. It was designed to be a nation under God, with liberty and justice for all. May it become a brilliant example of a nation that finds its way back to your heart. Chisel out the heart by removing rebellion and disunity so that it may have a clear motive set upon the lives of every leader. Raise up leaders in this generation that will be destined for your greatness and release your goodness over their lives. May wisdom visit our nation's leaders, citizens, and those who are here under your leadership. Restore protection over this nation's borders and put God back into every sphere of influence. It is and always will be your nation. We commit our nation to Christ's hands. AMEN.

BIBLIOGRAPHY

Benefiel, Dr. John. 2020. *Binding the Strongman Over America and the Nations.* Shippensburg, PA: Destiny Image Publishers, Inc.

Cordeiro, Wayne. 2007. *The Divine Mentor.* Minnesota: Bethany House Publishers.

Newton, Daniel T. 2021. *The Lost Art of Discipleship, God's Model for Transforming the World.* CA: Daniel Newton, Grace Place Ministries.

ENDNOTES

[1] https://www.washingtonpost.com/news/retropolis/wp/2018/06/14/the-gripping-sermon-that-got-under-god-added-to-the-pledge-of-allegiance-on-flag-day/

[2] For more information about the seven mountains of influence, see "Invading Babylon: The 7 Mountain Mandate" by Lance Wallnau and Bill Johnson, 2013

[3] https://bibletruthpublishers.com/rhinos-ugly-and-mean/sidney-r-gill/wonders-of-gods-creation-volume-3/s-r-gill/la90581

[4] https://biblia.com/bible/esv/1-samuel/6/19-20

[5] https://biblehub.com/hebrew/5921.htm

[6] https://www.biblestudytools.com/dictionary/abinadab/

[7] https://www.christiancourier.com/articles/1500-what-is-the-meaning-of-ekklesia

[8] https://www.biblestudy.org/bibleref/meaning-of-numbers-in-bible/7.html

[9] https://www.womanofnoblecharacter.com/12-in-the-bible/

[10] https://womenfromthebook.com/2012/08/14/esthers-make-over-fit-for-a-queen/

[11] https://www.womanofnoblecharacter.com/esther-in-the-bible/

[12] https://www.faipublishing.org/articles/key-house-of-david

[13] http://www.elijahlist.com/words/display_word.html?ID=4601

[14] https://www.learnreligions.com/what-is-the-kingdom-of-god-701988

[15] https://www.historicintercessioncity.com/

[16] https://www.cityofws.org/2159/Moravian-Story

[17] https://romans1015.com/1896-shearer-schoolhouse-revival/

[18] https://churchofgod.org/about/a-brief-history-of-the-church-of-god/

[19] https://www.almanac.com/content/when-is-rosh-hashanah

[20] https://www.biblestudy.org/bibleref/meaning-of-numbers-in-bible/25.html

[21] http://www.bobjones.org/index.cfm?zone=/Docs/Gullivers/Travels.htm

[22] https://strivingfortruth.com/7-baptisms-bible/

[23] https://www.prayingscriptures.com/jerusalem.shtml

Milton Keynes UK
Ingram Content Group UK Ltd.
UKHW020922201123
432908UK00020B/2648